MW00510516

PRAISE FOR

THE EXERCISE OF PROPHECY

Truly awesome! This book is a prophetic voice that has embraced the loving nature of God and the season of grace that Jesus ushered in on the cross. The reader will clearly understand why prophetic judgment is not an option today and why God will not speak in a way that belittles or devalues a believer's life. Every word spoken in the name of God should be spoken in the hot pursuit of love and for lifting our head so we might gaze into the beauty of Father's tender, loving eyes.

Jack Frost
Shiloh Place Ministries

Graham Cooke's book, *The Exercise of Prophecy*, is destined to be one of the most practical tools the Holy Spirit will use to enrich and deepen the lives of many who desire to move more powerfully in the gift of prophecy. I love the way the book is structured and the very practical applications and readings at the end of the chapters. The sidebars telling the stories of great people in the kingdom of God who moved in prophecy after the apostolic age are a great encouragement to us who do believe God still speaks to His church. I am excited about this first of six books in this series that Graham will write. I will encourage its reading by the students at our Global

School of Missions, Church Planting and Supernatural Ministry. I consider Graham Cooke one of the most respected persons I know who not only has a prophetic gift, but who is in the office of a prophet. It will be hard to find a more practical book to help you grow in prophecy. Graham has walked through many rough seasons in his life, and I am proud to watch him live out his life with great integrity and faithfulness to the author of all prophecy. Graham has been faithful to continue to bear the testimony of Jesus which is the spirit of prophecy.

Randy Clark
Global Awakening

Once again, Graham Cooke delivers an extraordinary book on prophecy. His unique ability to communicate spiritual truth is refreshingly authentic and theologically sound. As one who ministers in the prophetic, I am indebted to the wisdom of years that Graham has put into this writing. *The Exercise of Prophecy* is truly a one-of-a-kind manuscript that reveals the heart and mind of one of the foremost prophets and thinkers in the church today. It is a must-read that will help you navigate through the deep waters of prophetic ministry.

Larry Randolph
Larry Randolph Ministries

I highly recommend Graham's new book. He has profound insights into the nature of the prophetic ministry and never loses sight of the practical application.

Jack Deere
Evangelical Foundation Ministries

Graham Cooke's writings and teachings always leave me hungering and thirsting for more—more of God, more divine revelation, more understanding of God's heart, ways and values. His writings whet my appetite for the deep things of the Spirit because the truths Graham presents come alive within my heart. *The Exercise of Prophecy* is full of divinely inspired, revelatory treasures—treasures that took years of searching, refining, and preparing to bring them as gifts to you, the reader. The richness of its contents reveals that the writer has truly paid a great price to pen its pages. I love this book!

Patricia King
Extreme Prophetic

In *The Exercise of Prophecy*, Graham Cooke has clearly articulated truth that is attainable and achievable. He demonstrates what is possible for those who are concerned to grow churches that announce and demonstrate the kingdom of God. Graham provides practical and incisive insight that releases a congregation to move forward together into who they are called to be. There is absolutely no doubt that this book will both initiate the way forward and build the future for churches that are intent on cultivating an appetite for God.

Peter McHugh
Senior Minister, C3Centre

I had hardly advanced into the first chapter when I ran smack into a classic Graham Cooke revelation. He wrote, "God is more interested in creating collaborative prophetic communities than He is in birthing a new generation of prophetic superstars." If this is so (and I think it is), then God will surely use the new book as a tool to shape the skills and disposition of a new generation of prophetic voices. This new generation will have the ability to collaborate with one another and the throne room in a manner that will build a canopy of agreement between heaven and earth. Asaph taught his musician sons how to flow in the prophetic anointing of David's tabernacle, and I believe Graham's counsel will tune the instruments of the sons and daughters that God is raising to flow in the prophetic tabernacle that covers us in these last days.

Lance Wallnau
Lancelearning Group

I received a new level of faith in the while reading this book. Graham reveals the intentionality of God's love and encouragement towards us, and makes it clear how we are to hear His voice, know His heart, and prophesy confidently.

Julie Anderson
Prayer for the Nations

There is a curious tendency in "Spirit-filled" church life to promote the giftings of the New Covenant Spirit in the context of what is really Old Covenant practice. No wonder that we struggle with certain anomalies. However, there is brilliant news! Graham Cooke's new book, *The Exercise of Prophecy*, is a significant and mature contribution to the prophetic teaching arena, and his approach is best summarized by his comment, "Any time someone receives a prophetic word, grace should explode in his heart." Well said! The rest of the book is consistent with that statement in both its well-developed content and easily implemented practical exercises. This book is worthy of wide endorsement and exposure. We need a healthy, life-giving approach to the understanding and practice of prophecy, and Graham manages to accomplish this extremely well.

David Crabtree

Senior Pastor, DaySpring Church, Sydney, Australia

I've always enjoyed Graham's writings and public ministry. His recent bite-size, interactive format is just in time for a faster thinking, activational and demanding generation. He makes me think and take time to pause with insights that act as keys, unlocking my own creativity. Keep those keys coming... let's see what treasures lie ahead!

Steve Witt

Edify Ministries International, Author of
Experiencing Father's Embrace

It's rare to find a prophet who can prophesy *and* train others to do the same! Graham's new book puts a rich treasure into the hands of the church, not just to understand the nature of the prophetic, but to develop a sensitive heart to the voice of God. When Graham first came to CFC 16 years ago, he prophesied many things which we are now walking in. But he also empowered us to develop the prophetic when he left. If you can't get Graham to come and visit you personally, then this book is a very close second! It imparts God's heart, has wonderful insights, is easily understood, and at the same time gives very practical instructions on how to develop the prophetic. I doubt there is a better book on the prophetic in print.

Paul Reid

Leader, Life Link Team, Christian Fellowship Church, Belfast

In Graham Cooke's new book, *The Exercise of Prophecy*, he outdoes himself, as I've come to expect. He continually amazes me with each line in this book. How can one man come up with so many quotable quotes? Wow! Based solely on Scripture yet lived out in his own life, the content of Graham's new book will walk you through the real purpose for prophecy today. This book is about transition in the prophetic gift currently operating and accepted within the church. So, use this as a primer for yourself, your friends, or even your own church group. You will never think of prophecy in the same way again!

Steve Shultz
The Elijah List

My personal acquaintance with this author makes my endorsement both a privilege and a responsibility. There are few voices in the realm of the prophetic dimension in which there would be the freedom to recommend a manuscript without reserve. Graham Cooke is one that has excelled in this needed realm. He has been given an unusual ability to remain biblically accurate and spiritually insightful while wrapping every instruction and expectation in the love of the Father. If your heart hungers to know and become involved in the prophetic dimension, don't hesitate to make this volume your very own.

Bob Mumford
Lifechangers

VOLUME ONE

1

THE EXERCISE
of PROPHECY

THE CENTRAL THEMES OF PROPHETIC SPEECH

Graham Cooke

THE PROPHETIC EQUIPPING SERIES

The Exercise of Prophecy was formerly known as *Approaching The Heart of Prophecy, Module One.*

BRILLIANT BOOK HOUSE

Published by Brilliant Book House LLC
PO Box 871450
Vancouver, WA 98687

www.brilliantbookhouse.com

Copyright © 2019 by Graham Cooke

Requests for information should be addressed to:
    Email: admin@brilliantperspectives.com

All rights reserved. No part of this book may be reproduced, stored in a retrieval system or transmitted in any form or by any means—electronic, mechanical, photocopy, recording, or otherwise—without prior written permission of the copyright owner, except by a reviewer who wishes to quote brief passages in connection with a review for inclusion in a magazine, newspaper or broadcast.

Unless otherwise indicated, all Scripture quotations are taken from The Holy Bible, New American Standard Version. Copyright © 1960, 1962, 1963, 1971, 1972, 1973, 1975, 1977, 1995 by The Lockman Foundation.

ISBN: 978-0-9896262-8-6

DEDICATION

Every believer needs to hear God speak. He does not speak to our head, because the logic in our brain can only hear in the same way as a world that requires reason and rationale to understand anything. God speaks to our spirit where He lives in us. His mindsets are always the place of new thinking and wisdom that requires reflection and agreement.

His words rise up from within our spirit into our conscious minds, bringing trust and faith to bear in our relationship with the Lord. As we hear Him, a way of transition from old to new opens up a pathway from the now to the next.

I dedicate this book to all people, everywhere, who are going through the process of transition. Transition is a journey into the bigness of God for you. In that series of steps, you get to experience a transformation that opens up the heavens and makes a way for you on earth. Never forget, it is the process that makes you rich, not the outcome.

ACKNOWLEDGMENTS

If it takes a village to raise a child, then it takes an army of people to take territory and to keep it.

I know people who know how to fight for something. They stand in the Presence of The Ones who remain undefeated since the beginning.

The church needs a household of faith. A relational habitation that empowers trust, growth and maturity.

The kingdom requires an army. A disciplined body of people who are fixed on objectives and have the focus of warriors who know how to win.

If we are to take cities for God and raise up rural regions to encounter fullness in the face of warfare; then we must build churches that can prevail in the strategies and tactics of God.

We need the paradox of both household and army in order to accomplish our Kingdom role in the earth.

Lord, up the type of leaders who can break the grip of the world, the flesh, and the evil one.

ABOUT THE COVER

While vetting dozens of potential cover designs for *The Exercise of Prophecy*, I was reminded of a truth consistent with my experience in the prophetic: sometimes the key to transformation is illuminated by a glimpse of our Beloved.

Trials and difficulty, when revealed by the light of His promise, become our path to breakthrough and inheritance. What once we considered a moment of "crisis" is instead bathed in the glow of triumphant possibility. When we allow ourselves to be revealed in the light of Christ, God's truest nature reaches through that light—heralding the presence of His truth, hope, love, and freedom.

May God's light be a warm comfort on your surefooted journey.

Dia Becchio, Design

Psalm 119:105 says, "Your word is a lamp to my feet and a light to my path." If it takes a village to raise a child, then it takes an army of people to take territory and to keep it.

TABLE OF CONTENTS

INTRODUCTION

And it shall come to pass afterward that I will pour out My Spirit on all flesh; your sons and your daughters shall prophesy, your old men shall dream dreams, your young men shall see visions. And also on My menservants and My maidservants I will pour out My Spirit in those days. (Joel 2:28–29)

THE WORLD CHANGED THE DAY the Holy Spirit fell on Jesus' remaining disciples in that famed upper room in Jerusalem. The Spirit of God, reserved in the Old Testament for a select few, had now been placed on anyone who sought and loved Christ. With that outpouring came the gifts of the Spirit. While once only a few could prophesy, suddenly everyone could.

I have been in the prophetic ministry since 1974. I began prophesying the year before. That's more than thirty years of sharing the love God has placed in my heart. Amazingly, I'm still learning—and I never want to stop. Every year, I understand something new about God and His ways. He never ceases to intrigue me.

More than a decade ago, my book *Developing Your Prophetic Gifting* was first published. It has been a greater success than I could have ever imagined. It has gone through many re-printings; several publishers have taken it up; it has been written in many, many languages; and it still is on the best seller list. And yet, the material I teach now is light years beyond that original manuscript. I have come a long way in the years since I wrote that first book. For one thing, I have taught countless prophetic schools during that time. As I work with students and emerging prophetic voices, I have had my own gift shaped and honed. "As iron sharpens iron, so a man sharpens the countenance of his friend," as it says in Proverbs 27:17. The people I have met have pushed me further into the things of the prophetic. They have challenged me to find fresh ways of equipping, explaining, and encouraging.

For several months, I have felt the Lord prompt me to rewrite *Developing Your Prophetic Gifting*, adding the material I have taught in my schools over the past ten years since it was published. This book is the first in a series of six that will more fully equip people longing to speak the words of God to those around them.

Following the unqualified success of the spirituality journals in the *Being With God* series[1], I have decided to develop this material into the same format.

Each book has assignments, exercises and meditations, which, if followed, will bring each individual into an experience of God within the context of the material.

Together, we will study the practical elements of hearing God, of moving in the Spirit, of knowing God's nature, and of representing His heart to someone else. We will learn how to be grounded in the love, grace, and rhythm of God. It is my prayer that these books will give you something fresh about who God wants to be for you. As you read the principles and illustrations within, I pray that you will be excited and inspired to venture further into what God has for you.

---

1   See www.brilliantbookhouse.com for more information

Prophecy comes when we have a burden to encourage and bless the people around us. There is no magic formula to prophesying; it all depends on our love for God. When we love Him fully, that love should spill over onto the people around us. Prophecy is simply encouraging, exhorting, and comforting people by tuning them into what God has for them. In every church in the world, there are people who need that life-giving word from God. These aren't just the individuals who are obviously struggling; some appear to have everything together. But God knows what's really going on.

A SMALL MIND IS INCOMPATIBLE WITH A BIG HEART

Everyone could benefit from a prophetic word, even those for whom everything is soaring. I love to prophesy over people who are doing really well. If we can target those people and increase their faith at a critical time, they can fly even higher in the things of the Spirit.

New Testament prophecy will be spoken through the context of the Gospel of Grace. Jesus has received the judgment of God for sin for all those who are living, to enable them to find repentance through the goodness and kindness of God.

Prophecy is now in the context of a family; a company of called out people who are learning together to become the beloved of God: the Bride of Christ. There is a new language in the Spirit to learn and the unity of the Spirit to maintain and enjoy, as a people together.

Of course, there are necessary tensions in all good relationships, and prophecy is not the way to resolve conflicts. Clearly, we need wisdom for those situations.

I believe strongly that the more encouraging, exhorting, and comforting prophecy we have, the better our churches will be. Blessing and encouragement stir up anointing. The more of this kind of prophecy we can have in church, the less we will need intensive, time-consuming pastoral care. People will actually be touched by God and come into the things of the Spirit themselves. Individuals will realize that, yes, they are loved personally by God. That kind of revelation will stoke up their faith in ways a counseling session never could.

WHEN THE CHURCH RUNS OUT OF ENCOURAGEMENT, THE WORLD RUNS INTO WICKEDNESS

I know I need that kind of encouragement every day from the Holy Spirit. I can't remember the last time I asked Him to encourage me and He didn't. He may not speak it out immediately, but He always meets me at the point of my greatest need. That's just who the Holy Spirit is and what He loves to do.

This book can help you go further in the prophetic than you have ever hoped. After all, *"Eye has not seen, nor ear heard, nor have entered into the heart of man the things which God has prepared for those who love Him"* (1 Corinthians 2:9).

The Exercise of Prophecy is not a quick read. I encourage you to take your time going through this book, reading slowly and with your heart, until you understand the themes and thoughts they contain.

Furthermore, don't neglect the exercises, case studies, and Bible readings included at the end of each volume — they are valuable practice tools, which will take the lessons taught and put them into practice in your life.

Throughout this book, I have included several sidebar articles about some of my prophetic heroes. These are people who lived after the Bible was finished being written, heard the voice of God for themselves, and did marvelous exploits for the Kingdom. I hope this will open your eyes to a few of the people who have gone before us.

I have also included some suggestions of resources that may help you further explore the themes contained in this book. I hope they prompt you to dig deeper into the things of the Spirit.

Blessings on your journey into the prophetic!

Graham

1

THE EXERCISE
of PROPHECY

THE CENTRAL THEMES OF PROPHETIC SPEECH

VOLUME ONE
The Exercise of Prophecy

WHAT YOU WILL LEARN IN THIS SEGMENT:

- To develop confidence in God for your own journey.
- Prophesying for the common good
- Developing self-control in your language.
- The pursuit of love as a prime response to life.
- To represent the New Covenant in prophecy.
- Judgment is replaced by admonition and exhortation.
- To be in tune with the heart of God.
- Moving in the opposite spirit to what comes against us.
- Become a model of grace and truth.
- To be an ambassador for reconciliation.
- Freedom as a core doctrine of the prophetic.
- Develop your life message concerning the nature of God.
- Cultivate a great perception of God.
- Speaking what could be!
- Central themes of prophetic speech.
- Only humility restores people. Judgment comes back on you.
- How to perceive and use grace growers.

VOLUME ONE
The Exercise of Prophecy

WHAT YOU WILL LEARN IN THIS SEGMENT:

- The objective affects the delivery.
- Hypocrisy is always disciplined.
- The diagnosis and prognosis of prophecy.
- Prophesying the solution not the problem.
- Treasure seeking in the Kingdom.
- Discernment aids direction in proclaiming breakthrough.
- The difference between a grace issue and a discipline issue.
- Moving in the peace of God rather than the pressure of man.
- Dealing with frustration.
- Seeing in the Spirit.
- The difference between personal and private prophecy.
- Working with building and blessing prophets.
- Case studies in the prophetic.
- Recording prophecy is vital.
- Exercises and Assignments to help you grow.
- What contributes maturity and immaturity in the practice of prophecy.
- How to develop a partnership with leaders in this context.

THE EXERCISE *of* PROPHECY

GOD IS IN THE BUSINESS of developing prophetic companies around the world. I believe He is more interested in creating these collaborative communities than He is in breeding a new generation of prophetic superstars. His heart is to bring the whole body of Christ under a prophetic umbrella. To live in Christ is to live in the prophetic nature of God. The revelatory gifting is part of God's DNA, implanted in us at creation.

We are made in the image of God (Genesis 1:26, 27). Jesus came to restore that broken image through His death and resurrection. Image counts for something in the Kingdom. All good prophets are concerned with restoring the Christ-like image to the church. All prophecy is connected to rebuilding God's image in the Body of Christ. This is why we build into the Spirit and not against the flesh. What we build up (edify of Christ) in the image of God will automatically remove the flesh from the life of the believer.

Man has an inbuilt capacity to be drawn towards revelatory insight whether they are in Christ or not. It is part of the DNA in all people that they are drawn to the supernatural. It is the image of God. The Father did not remove His DNA because man had sinned. All people are made in His image. Until Christ reforms it, that image is fractured, but it still contains the propensity for spiritual experiences beyond the natural realm. If not Christ, then another power will seek to usurp that God-shaped vacuum in all people.

A church that denies the Holy Spirit and His presence and power is simply not able to compete in a postmodern culture where the organ for receptivity of truth is the eye and no longer the ear. People are not open to hearing about God. They want to see God at work because they live in a show-and-tell world.

Every one of us in the church has the capacity to prophesy. We can be a prophetic statement of what the Kingdom of Heaven is — showing people what Christ is really like — by our lifestyle, our actions, our thoughts, and our identity. We're a prophetic voice of

PROPHECY IS IN OUR DNA BECAUSE...

who God is, how He speaks, and what He's doing on the earth. We cannot help but be prophetic; it is in our very bones. It is who God made us to be.

It seems to me that the whole earth is waiting for something to be revealed. I sense that very clearly in my spirit; God wants to reveal something in these days that the earth has never seen. He is acutely interested in creating prophetic companies of people willing to hear His voice. He wants to finish better than we started — Pentecost was a wonderful beginning for the gifts of the Spirit, but God has even more in store.

Of all the billions of people walking the earth today, I believe that Christians should be the most confident. And out of that confidence should flow courage and boldness. We all need confidence for ourselves, to enable us to walk with God effectively and to overcome the world, the flesh and the devil. Prophecy is centered on restoring confidence, trust and faith to everyone who has an ear to hear. God wants a bold people, a prophetic company of declaration and proclamation. For far too long, the Church has been a people of explanation. God has not put us here to explain Him; He doesn't need our help, and we're not very good at rationalizing Him anyway. We can't explain Him, and we're certainly not supposed to apologize for Him. No, we are here to declare who He is. We are here to proclaim His majesty, and the best way to do that is by living it. Confidence is the lowest form of faith, but every Christian should stand at least at that level.

...WE ARE MADE IN THE IMAGE OF GOD

Prophecy can help build people's faith by revealing more of God's nature to them. In 1 Corinthians 12:4–7, we read more of the Holy Spirit's role in this:

Now there are varieties of gifts, but the same Spirit. And there are varieties of ministries, and the same Lord. There are varieties of effects, but the same God who works all things in all persons. But to each one is given the manifestation of the Spirit for the common good. (NASB)

That final phrase, "for the common good," is at the very heart of the revelatory gifts. The gifts of the Holy Spirit, including prophecy, are not just for our own personal benefit; they enable us to benefit the Church for the common good of everyone who is present. The gifts of the Spirit should never be abused—they are used only to bless the common good. The gifts of the Spirit are for the purpose of releasing and expanding the Kingdom not just empowering the church. The "common good," therefore, is about the benefit for all humanity and not just believers in Christ. Prophecy, as much as all aspects of Christ's spirituality, has relevance for all people, everywhere, at all times.

When God is vague about something, it is always for a purpose. Clearly, here He does not want us to know specifically what the "varieties" are of gift, ministry and effects. If He had specified exactly what these different varieties were, then humanity would have locked up the experience to only those elements. This is an invitation to be open in our thinking and practice. It is an ongoing call to intentionally explore the heart of the Father for all people and all circumstances. It is a summons to live a life of sensitivity to the Holy Spirit so that He may always give us not only the best gift, but the most suitable expression of it to that individual or people group.

Jesus only mentioned the word "church" two or three times in Scripture, but mentioned the "Kingdom" almost eighty times. He clearly wanted to keep our understanding of the Church as fluid as possible. *Ekklesia*, the Greek word for "church", means more than just a simple gathering; it can also mean a company of called out people. We are a committed band of people, meeting together for a common purpose. Church is not a place we go to. It is who we are together.

God didn't list the full variety of gifts because there are endless ways He can do things. He knew that if He had laid everything out for us, we would stop exploring the Spirit and quit experimenting with His gifts. In the past thirty years, I have worked with eighteen different kinds of prophets. I am sure there are more — I just haven't met them yet. I love discovering what kind of prophet a person is, and what the nature of their particular calling includes. God is not one-dimensional. He is multidimensional and far bigger than anything we could dream of.

OLD TURNS NEW

In 1 Corinthians 12–14, the Apostle Paul took great care to teach us how to use the vocal gifts. Three passages are particularly important to this study:

For to one is given the word of wisdom through the Spirit, and to another the word of knowledge according to the same Spirit; to another faith by the same Spirit, and to another gifts of healing by the one Spirit, and to another the effecting of miracles, and to another prophecy, and to another the distinguishing of spirits, to another various kinds of tongues, and to another the interpretation of tongues. But one and the same Spirit works all these things, distributing to each one individually just as He wills. (1 Corinthians 12:8–11)

If I speak with the tongues of men and of angels, but do not have love, I have become a noisy gong or a clanging cymbal. If I have the gift of prophecy, and know all mysteries and all knowledge; and if I have all faith, so as to remove mountains, but do not have love, I am nothing. (1 Corinthians 13:1–2)

Pursue love, yet desire earnestly spiritual gifts, but especially that you may prophesy. For one who speaks in a tongue does not speak to men but to God; for no one understands, but in his spirit he speaks mysteries. But one who prophesies speaks to men for edification and exhortation and consolation. One who speaks in a tongue edifies himself; but one who prophesies edifies the church. Now I wish that you all spoke in tongues, but even more that you would prophesy; and greater is one who prophesies than one who speaks in tongues, unless he interprets, so that the church may receive edifying. (1 Corinthians 14:1–5)

The vocal gifts of the Holy Spirit must lead us to do two things: pursue love and do everything for the purpose of edifying the body of Christ. We are to build each other up in every way possible. New Testament prophetic people are called, just like every Christian is, to be an ambassador for Christ: *"Now then, we are ambassadors for Christ, as though God were pleading through us: we implore you on Christ's behalf, be reconciled to God"* (2 Corinthians 5:20). As part of that call, we must represent the heart of God to people around us. We must give evidence of the essential nature of who God is within the New Testament covenantal relationship He has with us.

We cannot escape the new covenant; it is who we are. We have to represent that new covenant in every single thing we do. John the Baptist was the last of the Old Testament type of prophets, sent to prepare the way for Jesus. Christ was the first of the New Testament series of prophetic figures. John's mission was to bear witness to the arrival of a Messiah who came as prophet, priest, and king. Jesus Christ was that individual.

In Himself, Jesus taught how the prophetic was to be refashioned and remodeled in the new covenant. In His revolutionary Sermon on the Mount in Matthew 5–7, He repeatedly used the phrase, *"You have heard that it was said to those of old… but I say to you."* He knew the things He taught were causing controversy and consternation, because they

THE FATHER SEES YOU IN THE FUTURE AND...

were pushing a culture out of its Old Testament thinking and into a new day with God. Where once only a few could interact with God, now all would be able to.

In the Old Testament, we see a prophetic concentration of the gift in only a few people who represented the Lord. In the New Testament, we discover a prophetic distribution of the gift because now the Holy Spirit lives in all God's people who have surrendered to Him. Jesus said *"My sheep know my voice"* (John 10:3,4,16,27)!

This does not make everyone a prophet, that is a specific calling. However, we have all been given a lifestyle that involves communion verbally. It is impossible to build a successful, dynamic relationship with God if we cannot hear His voice. In chapter 10, John puts forth the truth that we can know by hearing and, therefore, not just by knowing scripture or the witness of friends.

Paul's statement that *"I wish even more that you would prophesy"* (1 Corinthians 12:5) resounds as strongly today as in the early Church. God's intentionality is part of His divine nature, unchanging and eternal.

Jesus wanted to prophesy because He loved to edify, exalt, and comfort. He shared the same passion for encouragement and tenderness that God the Father has. God is constantly looking at each of us, planning ways in which He can build us up. He loves us deeply, and has called us to pursue that same love.

To properly release the prophetic gift in our lives, we must remain in the love of God. We have to learn how to see people the way God sees them. Then we need to learn how to speak to them the way God would speak to them. Our interaction with people should cause them to understand and appreciate who God is and who He wants to be for them.

...LOVES TO SPEAK TO THAT IN YOUR PRESENT

When God speaks, it is an event. Something is created and birthed. Something is supposed to happen in people's hearts when they receive a prophetic word or action. *"Let your speech always be with grace, seasoned with salt, that you may know how you ought to answer each one,"* Paul taught in Colossians 4:6. *"Let no corrupt word proceed out of your mouth, but what is good for necessary edification, that it may impart grace to the hearers,"* he added in Ephesians 4:29. We are taught to put away malice, anger, wrath, slander and abusive speech from our mouth (Colossians 3:8). We are enjoined to pursue the things that make for peace and the building up of one another (Romans 14:9). We are commanded to speak whatever is true, noble, just, pure, lovely and of good report (Philippians 4:8). Our conversation—whether "everyday" or what we would term "prophetic"—must operate from the same grace base. This was the shift Jesus brought to the realm of the prophetic.

PROPHECY AND GRACE

God punished Jesus for the sins of the world because Christ made Himself available for judgment as we read in Romans 8:31–34:

What then shall we say to these things? If God is for us, who is against us? He who did not spare His own Son, but delivered Him over for us all, how will He not also with Him freely give us all things? Who will bring a charge against God's elect? God is the one who justifies; who is the one who condemns? Christ Jesus is He who died, yes, rather who was raised, who is at the right hand of God, who also intercedes for us.

SAINT FRANCIS
OF ASSISI

LIVED: 1182 to 1226

PROPHETIC SYNOPSIS: Born the son of a wealthy merchant, Francis turned his back on his former life when he heard God tell him to "Go, Francis, and repair My house, which as you see is falling into ruin." Francis followed this revelation and worked to fix a rundown local church. Despite being mocked and beaten, Francis kept building the little church by lugging huge stones and putting them in place. He did indeed fix that chapel—even at the cost of his relationship with his greedy father.

In 1208, Francis was touched by a sermon on Jesus sending out the disciples without money or extra clothing. He took that command to heart and gave away his remaining goods. Others joined him as he rebuilt several churches. Eventually, the Franciscans became their own Catholic order.

He traveled and preached, following his famous creed — he spoke the Gospel always, but only used words when necessary. His love for nature became legendary, and he wrote the magnificent Canticle of the Sun: "Most high, all powerful, all good Lord! All praise is Yours, all glory, all honor, and all blessing. To You, alone, Most High, do they belong. No mortal lips are worthy to pronounce Your name."

KEY COMMENT: "O Divine Master, grant that I may not so much seek to be consoled as to console; to be understood as to understand; to be loved as to love."

MORE: Read The Little Flowers of Saint Francis of Assisi by Saint Francis of Assisi

---

Source: St. Francis of Assisi. *The Little Flowers of Saint Francis of Assisi*, trans. Thomas Okey (New York: Dover Publications, 2003).

God delivered Jesus up for all of us, and now no one can bring a charge against us. As prophetic people, we must carry that same positive outlook. We represent the essential nature of God,

WE LIVE IN A PROPHETIC SEASON OF GRACE

including the Galatians 5 fruit of the Spirit. Being prophetic does not exempt us from being Christ-like. It doesn't mean we live one way and talk another. We don't get to live lovely in Christ but talk nasty in the spirit. Instead, we must display the character of God—loving, kind, gentle, patient, peaceful, joyful, good, and meek. Perhaps the hardest fruit for a prophetic person to show is self-control. Yet self-control is the only form of control that is acceptable in Church life. This is the basis for all true maturity, purity and integrity. People must take responsibility for how they speak in every circumstance. If the fruit of self-control is not visible in a person's life, then it is hard to trust the character of the one speaking.

In the New Testament Church, there is no place for judgment. When someone sins, they have an advocate in Jesus. We cannot bring charges against each other or we fly in the face of grace. *"My little children, these things I write to you, so that you may not sin. And if anyone sins, we have an Advocate with the Father, Jesus Christ the righteous,"* says 1 John 2:1–2. *"And He Himself is the propitiation for our sins, and not for ours only but also for the whole world."* The prophetic ministry points to that advocacy. While there is a place for correction, discipline, and chastisement, judgment must be thrown out of the equation. We read more about this in 1 John 4:7–11:

> *Beloved, let us love one another, for love is from God; and everyone who loves is born of God and knows God. The one who does not*

love does not know God, for God is love. By this the love of God was manifested in us, that God has sent His only begotten Son into the world so that we might live through Him. In this is love, not that we loved God, but that He loved us and sent His Son to be the propitiation for our sins. Beloved, if God so loved us, we also ought to love one another.

A truly prophetic voice is very in tune with the heart of God. Our role in the earth is to proclaim His love, seeing people as God sees them — not how we see them in the natural. Prophets speak to the all-sufficiency of Christ for people. We represent who God is in word and deed.

We are not subject to judgment because God has already judged Jesus. We are in a prophetic season of grace. God judged Jesus on the cross and He will judge us when the books are opened in eternity. Between then and now, however, we live in a season of grace. There **WAS JESUS PUNISHED ENOUGH? IF THE ANSWER IS YES, THEN…** is no judgment now, only the chastisement and discipline that comes because we are maturing into full sons and daughters of God.

Every day, the Holy Spirit is trying to bring us into cooperation with the Father. He has a series of adjustments He wants to make in our lives because He loves us. Unfortunately, there are times when those adjustments go unnoticed; we ignore them, but they don't go away. Many times, we just wait out the will of God rather than change.

Discipline that is not adhered to doesn't go away; it accumulates. It grows to a point where God has to chastise us. We can ignore discipline, but it will not ignore us. Eventually, it reaches the level where

God has to practically beat the living daylights out of us because He loves us so much.

...THERE IS NO JUDGMENT IN LIFE ONLY... When a handyman lays a floor, he knows the first row of tiles is the most important. If those are off even slightly, the floor will look worse and worse as he continues to build it. Eventually, it has to be completely redone. By ignoring God's call to realign that first row of tiles, we end up having to have our entire life pulled up and re-laid. Sensible Christians know this and keep a short account with God. They constantly repent for their sin and open themselves to His subtle touch. Hundreds of small adjustments are better than six really big changes. Being taken behind the woodshed by God is never fun. Discipline and chastisement are a part of our spiritual journey because they show that God loves us, that He wants us to change, and that there is no judgment for us now. So-called prophecies that are centered on sin, judgment and death tell us nothing about the nature of God but may reveal everything about the person prophesying! It is a significant witness to their lack of relationship with God. It witnesses to their inability to live, move and speak out of the fruit of the Holy Spirit (Galatians 5:22–26). It demonstrates the poor quality of their love and attitudes towards people.

In the New Testament, judgment becomes a sober assessment of what is right and wrong. Judgment does not always imply condemnation in the Bible. When used in relation to scriptures, it consistently refers to the evaluation of a believer's work in the context of them gaining reward from the Father (1 Corinthians 3:10–15).

God is not looking for opportunities to destroy people but to reveal His own nature to the earth. He is merciful. He is kind. He is good. It is the goodness and the kindness of God that leads us to repentance

(Romans 2:4). Jesus ever lives to make intercession (Hebrews 7:25). The whole world now belongs to the Father because the spirit of redemption has been released through Calvary. We are now God's prime ambassadors of reconciliation.

We are His visual aid to the earth to demonstrate the Kingdom of Heaven and to reveal the name and nature of God to a sin-sick and hurting world.

There is a rising tide of evil in the earth and there is no rising tide of goodness to combat it. "*We overcome evil with good*" (Romans 12:21). What if the problems in the world are not lawlessness and crime; not poverty and sickness; not greed and selfishness; not drugs or terrorism; not abortion or immorality? What if the biggest problem in the earth is simply the lack of goodness?

The ambassadors of Christ are spewing out judgment in the name of righteous indignation and the world is going to hell because we have misunderstood the glory of God.

...THE LAW OF SOWING AND REAPING AND...

When Moses asked to see the glory of God, the Father showed him His goodness while proclaiming His compassion. The world is wanting to know what God is like. Jesus came to put a face on God, the Church is present to put a face on Christ. *"He who has seen Me, has seen the Father."*

Millions of people are caught up in bondage. Many, many millions more are victims of evil and are living with no perception of the majesty of God's goodness. The sex slave trade is greater now than at any other time in history. Child abuse is at an all-time high. Poverty has never been worse in the history of man. More wars have been fought in the past century than ever before. Where is the goodness of God?

Where is the Church? Why are the people of God consumed by judgment and negativity when they should be leading lives overwhelmed by the goodness and the kindness of God? The Good News must become the Good News in our lives. The Church is an agent of freedom. It is for freedom that Christ has set us free. Not just our own freedom, but that of every living soul. We are caught up in a war between darkness and light. We are not fighting people but dark forces arrayed against us that persist in their intention to enslave all God's creation. Let us preach the gospel of reconciliation and the goodness of God to all men, everywhere, while at the same time taking authority in the name of Jesus over principalities and powers, and interceding for the victims living in fear and bondage.

Christians must live and operate within the nature of God. We must demonstrate the fruit of the Spirit. We cannot function outside of His lovingkindness and mercy. Indeed, when James and John asked for the fire of judgment, Jesus rebuked them gently: "*You do not know what kind of Spirit you are of*" (Luke 9:54–55).

...JUDGE AND YOU WILL BE JUDGED

There is a difference between a judgmental spirit and the Spirit of God, as seen in the face of Christ the Redeemer. We live in an age of redemption and we must live in that Spirit. The Old and New Testament anointings, particularly with regard to the prophetic, are manifestly different.

How do we maximize grace and mercy without reducing all forms of sin to a misdemeanor? There are some heinous sins being committed across the earth that clearly cannot be ignored. The Church must understand her role in the earth. Firstly, to act as ambassadors of grace and mercy through reconciliation (2 Corinthians 5:18–19). Secondly, to expose sin and to release people from bondage. "*Mercy triumphs over judgment*" (James 2:13). Unless it triumphs in the heart of each individual believer, they will never know the fullness of God's presence.

God comes to our perception of Him or not. When Jesus asked the question: "*Whom do people say that I am*" (Matthew 16:13), He was wanting to know about people's perception. From people's perception of us, we can gauge how we are going to be received. The Father builds the Church on the right perception of Him. We apprehend what we perceive, whether that is good or bad.

If we perceive God to be harsh, demanding, and prone to judgment, then our experience of Him is not going to grow into any great place of relationship. How do you make friends with a tyrant? It is impossible, because fear governs the relationship. Fearful of making mistakes, of saying the wrong thing, of doing a wrong act? Paranoia rules and peace is impossible.

However, if we perceive that the Father has huge wells of compassion and mercy, which never run dry... If we know Him as being One who is full of grace, rich in love, and abounding in love and truth... If He is slow to anger and incredibly patient toward us... If He is joyfully happy, with a sunny disposition... If His very cheeriness can cover the world... If He is scandalously forgiving and generous... If He is the very epitome of goodness; so much so that we can only be transformed when we link our repentance with His goodness and kindness... If *all* these things are true, and form a large part of the practical and spiritual theology of our life, then our whole personality is formed by such values.

Jesus was always accused of lavishing too much time on sinners (Matthew 9:11–13) and always had an answer for the religious people. God desires love and compassion in His people.

We are called to pray not to condemn. We are called, as Jesus is, to intercede for a depraved world to the God who cares. God takes care of His own wrath, He does not need our help. We have favor to request mercy (1 Timothy 2:1–2). The Father wills that all people should be saved. In that case, we must declare the goodness and kindness of God so that repentance may come (Romans 2:4).

Jeremiah knew the goodness of God and he also understood the prophetic role in a country where the One True God was not worshipped. It is to seek the good of the place where God has sent you, and to pray on behalf of its inhabitants. Blessing comes to blessing (Jeremiah 29:7).

Judgment comes to judgment (Matthew 7:1). We are told numerous times to pray *for* people, not against them. We have the honor of praying in line with the Holy Spirit's revelation of the Father. Therefore, we can appeal favorably to His compassion and mercy, which never fails (Lamentation 3:21–23), for they are daily renewable. The God who has always identified with sinners is unchanging in that respect. Read Isaiah 53 in order to understand the Christ-like nature. Jesus always opposed the spirit of the Pharisee by moving in the opposite spirit Himself. We must choose between being Christ-like and becoming a Pharisee. Jesus numbered Himself with sinners.

In our thinking, we must focus on mercy and grace or we will be mentally judging others. Jesus is "with us" and He is "for people." Pharisees define themselves by what they are against, thus putting themselves on the wrong side of God.

Jesus' appeal to the Church is to "*be merciful, just as your Father is merciful*" (Luke 6:36).

We are in a prophetic season of grace so, prophetically, let's be gracious. It is God's kindness and goodness that lead people to repentance, not our hammer of revelation. God's love is impossible to resist. To communicate it properly, our hearts have to be soaked in that love. We need to be completely overwhelmed by the grace of God.

Like any other secular group/organization, the Church today contains people who are skilled at running off at the mouth. We criticize one another, saying nasty, sarcastic, and disrespectful things. We ignore God's command that our ordinary speech be full of grace. We talk trash all week and then sing praises on Sunday. Such a lifestyle smacks of immaturity and a lack of self-control.

We all have choices to demonstrate our allegiance either to Christ or ourselves. There will always be difficult, hard-nosed people seeking to put their mental, emotional, and spiritual imprint upon our lives. How we move in the Spirit in those

EVERY SITUATION IS ABOUT WHO YOU CHOOSE TO BE IN THAT CIRCUMSTANCE

situations will tell an awful lot about us. What comes out of our mouth either glorifies the Father or defiles our heart and ministry. When we are trapped in a situation where people are being nasty and negative, we can choose to be Christ-like. If we don't choose the path Jesus would have taken, I guarantee that such sin will show up and influence our ministry. That negativity will be reflected in the way we prophesy. Our everyday conversations must have the flavor of God in them.

"For out of the abundance of the heart the mouth speaks," Jesus said in Matthew 12:34. It is great to worship and have our hearts filled with the presence of God. But what fills our hearts when we're in a negative situation: is it bitterness, sarcasm, or something cynical? It is in those

moments that we can win only by exercising self-control. We have to be better than we have been. We have to become Christ-like, for it is in those situations that our prophetic voice is established. It is so important that we develop a lifestyle of moving in the opposite spirit to what comes against us.

In tough situations, we must ask God what the need of that moment is. Do we need something? Does the other person need something? Instead of speaking out the first nasty comment that jumps to our minds, we must settle into the Spirit of God and speak a word of edification. If we can get into a lifestyle of gracious speaking in our everyday conversations, our prophetic ability will grow in leaps and bounds. The heartbeat of God will become clearer and clearer to us.

"But now you yourselves are to put off all these: anger, wrath, malice, blasphemy, filthy language out of your mouth," Paul wrote in Colossians 3:8. How could God be any more obvious than this verse? We must put those evil behaviors away and live a life of grace in word and deed. A prophetic voice cannot speak love and kindness one breath, and hate and bitterness the next; a fountain cannot give out both sweet and salt water. Being prophetic requires a tough choice about our lifestyle of communication. What will we speak out? No one can say ungodly things in conversation and expect to prophesy at a meaningful level. God will not honor such hypocrisy.

Our ordinary conversations show the Holy Spirit if we can be trusted with something remarkable. *"Therefore let us pursue the things which make for peace and the things by which one may edify another,"* says Romans 14:19. Perhaps the most famous passage in Scripture on this theme is found in James 3:8–12:

But no one can tame the tongue; it is a restless evil and full of deadly poison. With it we bless our Lord and Father, and with it we curse men, who have been made in the likeness of God; from the same mouth come both blessing and cursing. My brethren, these things ought not to be this way. Does a fountain send out from the same opening both fresh and bitter water? Can a fig tree, my brethren, produce olives, or a vine produce figs? Nor can salt water produce fresh.

If we do not tame our tongue, our gift will hit a glass ceiling and level off. Operating in the prophetic takes two things: we must trust God with everything, and He must bring us to the place where He can trust us. We can aspire to higher and deeper levels of the prophetic, but the cost of that is controlling our everyday conversations.

JESUS: THE MODEL OF GRACE

Jesus was full of grace and truth, and the perfect example for Christians to follow. Prophecy and grace must come together in our lives as they did in Christ's. *"Finally, brethren, whatever things are true, whatever things are noble, whatever things are just, whatever things are pure, whatever things are lovely, whatever things are of good report, if there is any virtue and if there is anything praiseworthy—meditate on these things,"* wrote Paul in Philippians 4:8. Jesus did just that: concentrated on truth, justice, nobility, purity, love, and virtue. He was unbelievably kind.

God understands our struggle in this because Jesus was wonderfully human, as we read in Hebrews 4:14–16:

Therefore, since we have a great high priest who has passed through the heavens, Jesus the Son of God, let us hold fast our confession. For we do not have a high priest who cannot sympathize with our weaknesses, but One who has been tempted in all things as we are, yet without sin. Therefore let us draw near with confidence to the throne of grace, so that we may receive mercy and find grace to help in time of need.

PROPHECY PROMOTES CONFIDENCE   No one reading this book has the burning desire to be the worst Christian who ever lived. But do many of us have a plan to be the best one? In all of our hearts, we have a hunger to be Christ-like. We want to be significant in the spiritual realm. The prophetic anointing allows us to see this desire in other people. It doesn't just tap into God's heart, but it lets us see others as God sees them. We can see the hunger, purity, and loveliness of another person. We can see their earnest desire for God.

Prophetic ministry is about drawing out of people what God has already put in them. Christ understands our weaknesses, for He too was human. Because of that fact, we can approach His throne of grace boldly. The prophetic word presents people with grace and truth. The truth about grace and the grace to be truthful with a real impartation of love!

Confidence in Christ is the only antidote for inadequacy and insecurity. When we learn who He is, our doubts about ourselves fade. We know that His grace is sufficient for us, and that we can enter His presence because we belong there. We can come before His throne with boldness because it is the very place where we receive mercy. By coming to Him, we gain the grace we need to face any situation in life.

New Testament prophets release individuals to that same place of confidence. When a true prophet ministers, no one is afraid. Instead, confidence in God builds within the listeners. Those who hear start to see God as He really is and begin to fall in love with Him all over again. The grace of God is intoxicating and irresistible. Prophets help inspire people to obtain mercy and grace.

When the Holy Spirit convicts of sin, He always brings us the gifts of mercy, grace, righteousness and forgiveness. He uses these gifts to restore our fellowship in line with our relationship with God in Christ. The Father has put us into Christ (relationship); it is the work of the Holy Spirit to teach us to abide there (fellowship). Literally, to establish the Christ life and likeness in us. All prophetic input is towards the same purpose. Edifying (1 Corinthians 14:3–4) leads to the establishing of our identity in Christ Jesus.

It is important that we all understand this basic, but vital, truth about Christ and life in the Spirit. We cannot prophesy outside of that revelation—we prophesy within that power.

NEW PROPHECY FOR NEW TIMES

The New Testament form of prophecy started by Jesus was startling in light of what had come before it. In Acts 10, Peter was given a new paradigm of how God worked. When he saw that sheet come down from Heaven, filled with every manner of "unclean" animal, he was sickened. He refused to go anywhere with Gentiles like Cornelius because they were "unclean." Three

IN PROPHECY, GOD INVITES US TO SEE WHAT HE IS SEEING... IN CHRIST

times, God had to shake Peter's upbringing off him: *"What God has cleansed you must not call common"* (Acts 10:15).

God wanted Peter to see the Gentiles differently. All of his life, the burly fisherman had been taught to not go into a Gentile home, not mix with any of them, and certainly not eat with one of them. And suddenly, after decades of living like this, God told Peter that He wanted him to do all of those things. You can almost hear Peter's protests: "I don't do that sort of stuff, Lord. It's not kosher. You wrote the book on that, remember?"

"What God has cleansed you must not call common."

This was a major shift for not just Peter, but the entire Jewish culture. Acts 11 shows the hot water such a revolutionary act landed him in. The other disciples, Peter's dear friends and colleagues, couldn't believe their ears. Peter's comment to them is astounding! *"Who was I, that I could stand in God's way?"* (Acts 11:17). What Peter experienced in his connection with the household of Cornelius was revolutionary and mindset changing!

Every single one of us is going to go through a similar kind of mental shift. God will change our paradigm about something. It will be as difficult for us to accept as it was for Peter. As prophetic people, we share the Lord's burden for releasing people from whatever imprisons them.

It is for freedom that Christ has set us free. All people who prophesy, and those called to the prophetic ministry and the higher office of a prophet, are jealous for people to have life and freedom in Christ. They want to see a people of promise and power emerge who know their God and who are living in His fullness.

Prophetic input leads us into an experience of the faith, hope and love of the Lord. Prophecy should turn our hearts towards the love of God. Even if the word convicts of sin, there must be a clear call to repentance in God that brings renewal (Revelation chapters 2 and 3).

In Luke 4, Jesus came out of the desert full of the power of the Holy Spirit. He walked into a synagogue, picked up a scroll, and opened it to Isaiah 61. Just the fact that Jesus took the Scripture out of sequence must have shocked all who were present. After all, the Jews would pick up God's Word from where they ended the previous reading. Jesus wasn't terribly interested in sticking to such a tradition. He just turned to His life message and read:

> *"The Spirit of the LORD is upon Me, Because He has anointed Me To preach the gospel to the poor; He has sent Me to heal the brokenhearted, To proclaim liberty to the captives And recovery of sight to the blind, To set at liberty those who are oppressed; To proclaim the acceptable year of the LORD." Then He closed the book, and gave it back to the attendant and sat down. And the eyes of all who were in the synagogue were fixed on Him. And He began to say to them, "Today this Scripture is fulfilled in your hearing." (Luke 4:18–21)*

As prophetic people, we all need a life message about who God is and what He is like. Jesus' understanding of God the Father was that He loved the poor, brokenhearted, enslaved, oppressed, and sick. This call on His life focused His prophetic gift. He was constantly kind and generous to those whom He was called to help.

Jesus was full of grace and truth as a prophet. It's important that we are too; but truth by itself will only change people. Truth causes transformation when it is

PROPHECY CAN OPEN ANY PRISON DOOR

SAINT MARTIN OF TOURS

LIVED: 316 to 397

PROPHETIC SYNOPSIS: Martin was a young soldier when he came across a beggar at the gate to the city of Amiens, France. Gripped by compassion for the poor, freezing man, Martin tore his own cloak in two and handed it to the man.

That night, Martin had a vision of Jesus Christ dressed in the piece of cloak he had given to the beggar. Jesus smiled, looked at the angels around Him, and said proudly: "Martin... clothed me with this robe." Smiling, He quoted Matthew 25:40—"Inasmuch as ye have done it unto one of the least of these my brethren, ye have done it unto me."

That revelatory vision changed his life. Martin left the army and became a monk: "I have served you as a soldier; let me now serve Christ. Give the bounty to these others who are going to fight, but I am a soldier of Christ and it is not lawful for me to fight," he said. Once, a group of thieves robbed him—and he led one of them to Christ on the spot.

Throughout his life, Martin followed the insight given to him in his dreams. He used that gift to plan pilgrimages, trips, and moves. His contemporaries record that he operated strongly in the prophetic. Even in his final days—having known through a prophetic word that he was about to die—he traveled a long distance to reconcile two warring factions within a church.

KEY COMMENT: "Place me alone in the front of the battle, with no weapon but the cross alone, and I shall not fear to meet the enemy single-handed and unarmed."

Source: Bateman, Jordan. "The Mindfulness of St. Martin." *AWE Magazine*, Winter 2003, pp. 8–9

powered by grace. When those two spirits work together, they have an incredible effect upon humanity. It doesn't matter if the individual is Christian or pre-Christian, truth and grace affects them.

There is a difference between change and transformation. Change can seem a temporary alteration of behavior during a particular season. It could be that people drive their carnal behavior underground when confronted and then return to it when the heat is off.

Transformation occurs by the action of God's grace on truth when we allow the Father to touch our innermost place and we surrender life at that point. It is possible to have great truth but ruin it with poor grace. People then feel brow-beaten by the truth rather than seeing the beauty of what the Father is offering in Christ. Pharisees are inveterate bullies.

I am fascinated by the idea that Christ proclaimed His life message—"*The Spirit of the LORD is upon Me... to set at liberty those who are oppressed*"—to the Church of His day. He did not read from the scroll, or paraphrase it during His Sermon on the Mount, or when He fed the five thousand. He didn't tell the masses that He would save them, but He told the religious community. "*I'm going to release you from prison,*" He prophesied to them.

The Church of Jesus' day was locked in its religious, pharisaical prison. Its system had bred thousands of brokenhearted, oppressed captives. These people had to be freed, and Christ knew it.

OUR PERCEPTION OF GOD

What we think about God is the single most important thing in our lives. Whatever we perceive God's nature to be will color how we live

WHEN YOUR PERSONAL REVELATION OF GOD IS INCREASED, YOUR...

spiritually, physically, emotionally, and relationally. It is unavoidable. *"For the testimony of Jesus is the spirit of prophecy,"* says Revelation 19:10. Our testimony of who Jesus is for us will drive our prophetic gift for the rest of our lives. For better or for worse, how we connect with God's nature will determine how we prophesy.

In Exodus 33–34, Moses had a unique encounter with God. The Lord lovingly maneuvered Moses into asking for the very thing He wanted to give him. Because everything originates in God, we know that Moses' desire was placed there by Him. *"Please, show me Your glory,"* Moses asked in Exodus 33:18. In Heaven, God smiled. Moses had caught the very thing God wanted to give him.

God placed Moses in a small cleft in a rock. *"So it shall be, while My glory passes by, that I will put you in the cleft of the rock, and will cover you with My hand while I pass by,"* He said in Exodus 33:22–23. *"Then I will take away My hand, and you shall see My back; but My face shall not be seen."*

That experience changed Moses. As God walked past him in Exodus 34:6–7, He prophesied to Moses about Himself:

> *Then the Lord passed by in front of him and proclaimed, The LORD, the LORD God, compassionate and gracious, slow to anger, and abounding in lovingkindness and truth; who keeps lovingkindness for thousands, who forgives iniquity, transgression and sin; yet He will by no means leave the guilty unpunished, visiting the iniquity of fathers on the children and on the grandchildren to the third and the fourth generations.*

Suddenly, Moses had a whole new revelation of who God wanted to be for him.

God never changes. He is still merciful and gracious, and all of the other things He told Moses. But our ability to understand His character traits grows and deepens as we spiritually mature. The nature of God is constant, but we are not. That's why we need to spend time with Him, learning as much about His character as we can. Moses' burning bush experience paled in comparison to seeing the back of the Almighty. He had proven himself worthy and grown to the next level. He was changed by what he saw from the cleft in the rock; even his face glowed afterward.

I believe the world is ready for a revelation of who God truly is and what Christianity is really about. We're ready to come to a place of deep truth where the prophetic nature of God bubbles within us. God wants to give each of us a unique vision of Himself—sharing what He is like, what He loves,

...PROPHESYING GOES TO A WHOLE NEW LEVEL OF INTIMATE PROCLAMATION

what He sees, and what He dreams. This revelation is so profound that it will change the way we think forever. When we walk through dry places, it will sustain us. It is water for our spirits.

SPEAKING WHAT COULD BE

God always speaks to our potential. In Luke 19, we read that Zacchaeus, a much-loathed tax collector, was up in a tree trying to see Christ. He was an obnoxious person who had defrauded most of the community. Some say he may have been up the tree because he couldn't see over the crowd, but I think he was up there for security purposes as well. A crowd that big, full of people who hated him—it was just a matter of time before he took a knife between his third and fourth ribs.

Hiding in trees wasn't the life Zacchaeus had dreamed of. He yearned for more. He wanted to be loved and accepted. As Jesus walked through Jericho, He had the option to eat with anyone there. Everyone would have loved to have Him over for a meal—they would get to meet Him, and then brag to their friends afterward. So who did Jesus choose? The one man everyone hated.

"Zacchaeus," Jesus said in Luke 19:5, *"make haste and come down, for today I must stay at your house."*

That acceptance changed Zacchaeus's life. Jesus never prophesied his sin to him, but instead loved him. The fruit of the encounter was immediate, according to Luke 19:7— *"Look, Lord, I give half of my goods to the poor,"* Zacchaeus said. *"And if I have taken anything from anyone by false accusation, I restore fourfold."* Jesus merely filled Zacchaeus's need to be loved, and the rest flowed from that.

From one simple, positive act towards a loathsome individual, the whole village experienced a blessing. Money flowed into families that had been defrauded. It was like the whole village won the lottery!

It's amazing what can occur in a community when we suspend judgment in favor of blessing.

When prophetic people confront someone with their sin, they inevitably hold onto it. Without grace, the truth is useless. Our call is to speak to their potential.

It is important that our hearts are exercised in giving grace and mercy. *"Mercy and truth have met together; righteousness and peace have kissed,"* says Psalm 85:10. We need to live within that embrace, so that we can bear fruit according to Isaiah 32:17— *"The work of righteousness will be peace, and the effect of righteousness, quietness and assurance forever."* This is the very foundation of the Kingdom of Heaven: *"The kingdom of God is not eating and drinking, but righteousness and peace and joy in the Holy Spirit"* (Romans 14:17).

Righteousness and peace are two themes central to the prophetic gifting. Anyone who wishes to speak God's words must remember passages like James 3:17–18:

> *But the wisdom from above is first pure, then peaceable, gentle, reasonable, full of mercy and good fruits, unwavering, without hypocrisy. And the seed whose fruit is righteousness is sown in peace by those who make peace.*

THERE IS A BEAUTY IN THE LORD THAT IS AMAZING!

Hypocrisy is a major pitfall for many prophetically gifted people. The Bible assures us that hypocrisy will be disciplined. One needs only look at Romans 2:1–7 for evidence of that:

> *Therefore you have no excuse, everyone of you who passes judgment, for in that which you judge another, you condemn yourself; for you who judge practice the same things. And we know that the judgment of God rightly falls upon those who practice such things.*
>
> *But do you suppose this, O man, when you pass judgment on those who practice such things and do the same yourself, that you will escape the judgment of God? Or do you think lightly of the riches of His kindness and tolerance and patience, not knowing that the kindness of God leads you to repentance? But because of your stubbornness and unrepentant heart you are storing up wrath for yourself in the day of wrath and revelation of the righteous*

judgment of God, who WILL RENDER TO EACH PERSON ACCORDING
TO HIS DEEDS: *to those who by perseverance in doing good seek for
glory and honor and immortality, eternal life…*

When we despise the richness of God's goodness, forbearance and
longsuffering, then we open ourselves up to becoming Pharisaical and
judgmental.

Judgment has become part of the spirit of the age. The world acts
out its condemnation on the news channel with approval ratings. On
reality TV, people are voted out summarily by others with a vested inter-
est in taking their place. We have poll ratings for everything so that
everywhere people can execute their perceived right to judge another.

The justice of God does fall on people. When it does, it is not a pretty
sight. My advice to anyone playing with such a possibility is to stop everything and immediately repent. You don't want God's justice to smash
down on you. Like a rock falling from the sky, it will crush you. Severe
chastisement is not fun, enjoyable, or easy to recover from. Let go of your
stubbornness and ask God to soften you to His Spirit. In Matthew 7:1–5,
Jesus Himself is every bit as clear as Paul was on the sin of hypocrisy:

*Do not judge so that you will not be judged. For in the way you
judge, you will be judged; and by your standard of measure, it will
be measured to you. Why do you look at the speck that is in your
brother's eye, but do not notice the log that is in your own eye?
Or how can you say to your brother, "Let me take the speck out of
your eye," and behold, the log is in your own eye? You hypocrite,
first take the log out of your own eye, and then you will see clearly
to take the speck out of your brother's eye.*

With the same standard we use to measure people, we ourselves will be measured.

A friend of mine was once stuck in a bad church situation. It was a place where cynicism and criticism were in control. One day, a particular individual came to him and began tearing down other people in the church. Every time he started talking about someone, my friend would literally duck beneath him. When he would start attacking someone new, my friend would again duck. Finally, the man demanded to know what was going on.

"Why are you doing that?" he asked.

"That plank in your eye—every time you swing it around, I'm afraid it's going to knock my head off," my friend replied. What can I say? He has a strange sense of humor, but he did get his point across.

Brethren, even if anyone is caught in any trespass, you who are spiritual, restore such a one in a spirit of gentleness; each one looking to yourself, so that you too will not be tempted. Bear one another's burdens, and thereby fulfill the law of Christ. (Galatians 6:1–2)

People become inconsiderate when they fail to renew their own humility. We can only restore people when we are living our lives in a state of meekness before God. Meekness is not weakness, it is strength under control.

Beware, lest your truth have wrong companions, such as anger and not grace! If you enjoy putting people straight, you may need to examine your own heart.

Correcting people is an awkward process requiring great love, humility and fruit of the Spirit. Truth, when preceded by grace, will transform.

GRACE GROWERS

It's not easy to love everyone, but it is the call on every prophet's life. To test us in this, God deliberately puts people around us who are meant to be loved by us. Oftentimes, we will have to be very creative to love them; some of them, by design, are not easy to love. But those unlovable ones, ironically, teach us the most about God's heart.

I call people like these grace growers. They cultivate the grace in my life by forcing me to be intentional about loving them. In Luke 6:27–36, Jesus taught us about grace growers:

THE LORD CHOOSES SOME STRANGE PEOPLE TO CONVEY HIS HEART...

But I say to you who hear, love your enemies, do good to those who hate you, bless those who curse you, pray for those who mistreat you. Whoever hits you on the cheek, offer him the other also; and whoever takes away your coat, do not withhold your shirt from him either. Give to everyone who asks of you, and whoever takes away what is yours, do not demand it back. Treat others the same way you want them to treat you.

If you love those who love you, what credit is that to you? For even sinners love those who love them. If you do good to those who do good to you, what credit is that to you? For even sinners do the same. If you lend to those from whom you expect to receive, what credit is that to you? Even sinners lend to sinners in order to receive back the same amount. But love your enemies, and do good, and lend, expecting nothing in return; and your reward will be great, and you will be sons of the Most High; for He

Himself is kind to ungrateful and evil men. Be merciful, just as your Father is merciful.

I first learned about grace growers in the 1980's when I began doing schools of prophecy in the U.K. They were among the first of their kind, and so attracted a lot of attention, both positive and negative. There were several "ministries" that felt threatened by what I was doing, and there were various people who were totally convinced that training people to hear God's voice was demonic!

Three such men began to follow me around, convinced it was their calling from God to expose me and protect the body of Christ from my ministry. They genuinely thought that they had a mandate from God to oppose me and pull me down (John 16:2). They would **...YOU ARE PROBABLY ONE OF THEM!** visit cities where schools were booked and try to persuade pastors to warn their people not to attend. They would be outside the venues on the day, holding placards and handing out leaflets warning people. Then, they would come into the school, put their placards at the back of the hall, and sit in the front row directly in front of the lectern. They would take copious notes and afterward write a newsletter explaining the teaching and why I was a heretic. We called them the three stooges.

This went on for two years. They booked in to every school! I cried out to the Lord, "Please, kill 'em." Well, that prayer didn't work, so I modified it to maiming: "Lord cut off their writing hand... do something!"

Several weeks later, He answered my prayer, though not in the manner I had envisioned. One night, I had a dream. I am used to dreaming. Most of my revelatory dreams begin in the same way so that I am able to retain what I see, hear, and experience in the dream.

God is on His throne. I am sitting on one arm of it, with my legs over His lap, and our heads are together talking. In this particular dream, the Father had something to show me. When I readily agreed, He gave a command off to one side of His throne. An angel walked in with a huge block of the most beautiful marble I had ever seen. It was six feet high, four feet wide, and three feet deep. It was glorious and breathtaking.

Jesus came into view, smiling that lovely, slow, small smile of His. He dug a finger into the marble and made an outline of a figure in the stone. I watched, entranced. The Father asked, "Would you like to see it made?" I nodded enthusiastically and He gave a command. Three pairs of hands and arms (up to the elbow) appeared. Each pair held a hammer and chisel, and at the command of the Father, began sculpting this figure out of the marble.

"If you encourage them, they will work faster and it will be completed more quickly," He said, smiling at me. I began tentatively to bless and encourage them, but it didn't seem to make any difference. "My son, you must always be wholehearted in your encouragements," He said, laughing. I began to exhort, bless, and encourage loudly, encouraged by the Father. At one point, I was standing on the arm of His throne with my hand on the Lord's head (for balance!) shouting encouragement at the very top of my voice! Everywhere was pandemonium! There was huge laughter and cheering all around me. One angel was lying on the floor, beating it with his fists, and screaming with laughter. The draft of his wings almost knocked me off my perch.

Eventually, the work was finished and the noise became peace. I was exhausted and sank down to my original position. I stared in awe at the figure that had been created. "Do you know what it is?" the

Father breathed into my ear. When I shook my head, mute in awe and wonder, He turned my face to look in His eyes.

"It's how I see you, my son. It's the man I am making you into." I looked again at the figure and began to cry. "But it's so beautiful, my Lord," I whispered. He smiled gently, looking full into my face. "Would you like to thank the sculptors?" He asked with a smile. "Sure!" I said, turning back to the statue. My smile of thanks turned to one of total shock and horror when the three stooges suddenly appeared next to the sculpture. "Aargh!!" I screamed at the top of my voice; so loudly, in fact, that I woke myself up!

Suddenly, a flood of revelation filled my waking heart and mind. I began to realize the purpose of the Lord over the last two years. God allows, in His wisdom, what He could prevent by His power. All their opposition had driven me to strive to be an excellent teacher. Their criticism had pushed me into a place of continuously upgrading my material and the quality of presentation. School of Prophecy was gaining an excellent reputation because I had consistently upgraded it in the face of their antagonism. What had not been upgraded, I realized, was my own nature and character. Their hostility had not produced in me an opposite spirit that craved Christ-likeness. I had been offended, angry, and affronted. I had affected a grieved spirit, believing it was justice.

I had not at all seen that the purpose of the Father was also to change my character and personality. He was seeking to beautify me by making me like Jesus. I saw His plan and I wept. I cried because of my stupidity. Why could I not have foreseen His purpose early on in the circumstance? I began to understand that I valued my material and my ministry more than being made in the image of Jesus. I wept for that.

I saw the value that the Father placed on my becoming like Him. I resolved to change my ways with the help and support of the Holy Spirit. I resolved to put character transformation at the top of my list of responses to the workings of God.

GRACE GROWERS PROVIDE US WITH A SHORTCUT TO ENTER THE PRESENCE OF GOD AT A DEEPER LEVEL OF RESPONSE

I got it. I understood the purpose of grace growers. They were present in my life to teach me the grace that is currently mine to be made in the image of Jesus. Grace growers provide an unconscious opportunity (on their part) for us to experience a breakthrough in the image of God. I had only approached the situation from a functional and not a relational paradigm. Pride and vanity had made me change my product but not my heart.

My attitude changed. I thought through the effect that these men had on my outlook and my personality. Suddenly, all the clues were there to be seen; so obvious now. I was supposed to learn patience with joy; blessing and not cursing; how to love those who were in enmity; how to be kind and gracious in the face of unkind opposition.

The next months were vastly different. Now, I prayed positively for these guys. I had compassion, kindness and love for them. I lost my victim mindset. I ceased to be offended by their actions and became profoundly grateful to the Lord instead. I learned my lesson and it has been the foundation of all ongoing transformation since.

Grace growers are people you love to hate and who hate to love you. They are a gift of God to bring a pressing transformation to bear quickly on our lives. Better the grace grower you know, than the new one who will have to take their place!

God puts these people in our lives to teach us about being Christ-like. How do we love our enemy? By refusing to see him as such. We all have difficult people around us, but they are going to experientially teach us how to discover and explore the love of God. It will kill us to love some of them; such struggle cracks open our heart to the Holy Spirit. God wants us to look at His children with the same love He feels. The harder they are to love, the more God will pour Himself out on us to accomplish that action.

What a mystery this is! The very people we find the hardest to get along with can bring us the closest to Christ. To connect with some-one, we must see them as Jesus sees them. We have to look beyond the rubbish, "looking for the baby Jesus under the trash," as U2 sings. We must look beyond the brave fronts we all put up and see each other for who we truly are. When we see someone the way God sees them, we can speak to that treasure.

HOW PROPHECY STARTS

In prophecy, the first thing we need to receive is a sense of burden. When we give ourselves fully to God's love and grace, our hearts are tuned to the same wavelength as God's. We inherit a sense of owner-ship for the church community He has placed us in, and, out of the burden, God will express His heart.

We need to be intentional and look around where we live, ask-ing God, "Who, Lord, do You want to speak to in my church, on my street, or in my daily life? Lord, give me a burden." Once we receive that burden—or compulsion to pray for someone—we can explore it further by asking God several questions:

- What are You really saying through this burden?
- What are Your hopes and dreams for this individual?
- What is it You want me to do?
- At the end of this prophecy, what do You want to achieve in this person's life?
- What is Your objective?

We can never assume that we will immediately know all of the right answers. A strong sense of burden can take time to work through and explore with the Holy Spirit. But God will give us a sense of objective. To develop an understanding of how God's heart works towards people is very important. Why is He picking this person to receive prophecy? What does He want to achieve through this word?

Having a sense of God's objective helps us to be clear, specific, and significant in what we are prophesying. It is similar to what schoolchildren experience when they are taught how to write an essay: we must support and develop God's thesis, His key theme, for that person's life. Without a sense of objective, we sometimes fudge the words or pad the prophecy with too many human insights. We see a blurrier picture because we do not have a sharp focus on what God wants to do.

God's objective also affects our delivery: we must present the word in a manner that connects with whatever God wants to do. *"Most assuredly, I say to you, the Son can do nothing of Himself, but what He sees the Father do; for whatever He does, the Son also does in like manner,"* Jesus said in John 5:19. If God wanted to impart His peace to a person, you usually wouldn't grab the individual by the scruff of the neck and yell into

THE OBJECTIVE AFFECTS THE DELIVERY OF PROPHECY

his face: "Thus says the Lord, 'BE AT PEACE!'" If it was the Father's love that was to be shared, you probably wouldn't be harsh to a person. The objective and delivery cannot be at odds with each other, or there will be no impartation.

If the objective is to strengthen people, to add resolve and determination to their lives, our prophesying will reflect that aim. We will prophesy in a bold, forthright manner, dwelling on the supremacy of God and taking care to release a confidence into the people concerned. If we have received a word from the Lord about His love for an individual, we should communicate that in a way that causes God's love to be spread into that heart.

DIAGNOSIS VERSUS PROGNOSIS

When we receive a sense of objective, we then begin to focus in on what God wants to say to the individual. Often, the first thing we receive is diagnostic. A significant difference exists between a prophetic diagnosis and a prophetic prognosis. A diagnosis is the process of determining the nature and cause of a person's need. A prognosis is how God weaves Himself into that diagnosis. In medical terms, we can be diagnosed with the flu and given a prognosis of full health after a few days of rest, orange juice, and chicken noodle soup.

Sometimes, we can see a vision or have an intimation that is quite negative. We may see a fault, a wrong, or a sin. Often, this first impression is simply diagnostic. Prophecy is made up of three elements: word of knowledge, gift of prophecy, and word of

DO TO OTHERS WHAT YOU WOULD HAVE THEM DO FOR YOU

wisdom. A word of knowledge opens up the issue, a prophetic word speaks God's heart into it, and a word of wisdom tells us how to respond to God.

That first shred of negativity we sometimes get may actually be a word of knowledge, not a word of prophecy. God can give us information about a person's life in order to contextualize, for us, the prophetic word to come. "This is what is happening," God says. "I need you to understand it before it can be spoken into." God is telling us what He wants to overthrow next in that person's life (Jeremiah 1:10) so that He can build or plant something better.

Most people prophesy the first thing they receive. We can actually prophesy a word of knowledge that God gave us as information. It is called prophesying the problem and has probably damaged more people's lives than any other activity in the prophetic realm. Never give the first thing you receive; don't be in a hurry to prophesy. It's not a race. You are dealing with sensitive issues in a person and can hurt them greatly. We must not feel that we have to get a word out of our mouth as soon as we get it.

We must perfect the art of stepping back into our spirits when we receive revelation. We can dialogue with God when we receive that first impression. "Thank You, Father," I often say. "I understand that about his life. Now, in light of that, what is it You want to say to him?" What He gives us next could be the complete opposite of what we first saw because the grace of God may need to come into operation.

The word of knowledge, in many cases, is for diagnostic purposes. The Lord reveals the situation to us as it is at the moment. However, the prophetic word we give may relate to what the Lord is going to do both now and in the future. We can give the individual their prognosis. Diagnosis identifies what is, while prognosis indicates what is to come.

Context is incredibly important to God. When we receive a word of knowledge, we need to ask ourselves two questions:

- Is this word diagnostic?
- If so, is it for me personally, so that I can become familiar with the situation?

If the answer to both questions is "yes," then we have a context, or set of circumstances, into which God wants to speak. We need to use that privileged information wisely—being sensitive to the Holy Spirit and respecting the people concerned.

One of the hardest things for prophetic people to learn is that not everything that we receive is to be given. Many prophetic ministries speak out everything they see and hear from God, broadcasting a person's innermost fears and flaws to a packed auditorium. We must become constrained by love, and remember Jesus' golden rule: *"And just as you want men to do to you, you also do to them likewise"* (Luke 6:31). Prophesy the second thing you get.

SPEAK THE SECOND THING

I learned this principle for the first time in a Welsh church in 1986. God set out a precedent for me, and I have held fast to that ever since. My first evening there, I had dinner with a number of leaders. One thing led to another, and I ended up praying for some of the elders there. I prophesied over the pastor of the church—for the sake of this anecdote, I'll call him David. I was working my way around the room when I came to an elder named John. Touching his shoulder, I told him that I just wanted to wait on the Lord and see if God had anything He wanted to say. In my spirit, I asked God what He saw over John.

Immediately, the Lord showed me a picture of John holding an eighteen-inch-long knife in his hand. It was a wicked-looking blade, tapering from four inches wide at the hilt to a sharp point, and serrated on both sides. John took his knife and began stabbing the main leader, David, in the back over and over. He didn't do it just once or twice, he stabbed him twelve, fifteen, twenty times. He plunged the knife into David, trying to get it in as deep as it could go. From every conceivable angle, John stabbed David in the back. I was stunned, to be honest. I couldn't believe how vicious it was.

THE SPIRIT ALWAYS GIVES LIFE

I asked the Lord for an interpretation. "What's this all about?" I said to Him in my spirit. God showed me that John thought he should be the leader of the church. He thought he was more anointed, had a better ministry, and felt he was a better-equipped leader. In private, he took every opportunity to run David's ministry down. He sullied his reputation, his gifting, his style, everything. John desperately wanted to build a platform for himself; he wanted status and was profoundly jealous of David's popularity.

At that moment, to be perfectly honest, I felt a sense of dread. I was suddenly aware that what I did next was going to be incredibly important — not just for John, but for me. I stepped even further back into my spirit and asked God what I was supposed to do with this information.

Imagine if I had prophesied the first thing I saw! "John, thus saith the Lord: stop it, you backstabbing little rat!" I held John's life in my hands in those few seconds. I could either release him from what he was doing, or bring him to a place where he would be finished in that church. If I exposed him, no one in that room would ever trust him again. Those other leaders, and especially David, would have been wary of him. A stigma would be placed over his life because I exposed something that God wanted me to use only for diagnosis. He would have been humiliated. Of course, I would have come out looking great and wonderfully "revelatory." I could have rationalized away what I did to that poor man by saying, "truth is truth."

Yes, truth is truth. But there is also grace, compassion, and mercy that come with it. We can express God's desires in a way that does not water down the truth, but is also in line with His love for the individual involved.

In my spirit, I asked the Lord what he wanted to do. "How do I handle this? What am I supposed to say?" I asked. Instantly, the peace of God came over me.

"Grae," I felt the Lord say, "I want you to know what is going on in his life. But I want you to say something that is going to release him from that." If I had prophesied the problem, I would have locked him up for years. He would have been known as that backstabber for the rest of his life. I wouldn't have freed him; I would have turned him into a prisoner of other people's fears and perceptions. He would have had to move to a new city to be free.

Fortunately, God showed me exactly what to do. I asked John and David to stand up, back to back. I looked around and found an old broom handle, and placed it in John's hands.

"John, I want you to pretend this broom handle is a sword," I said. "The Lord has brought you two men together. He has stood you back-to-back, which is a fighting position. He is giving you a charge into your life, John, to guard David's back, to look after him because the enemy wants to have and destroy his life and pull him down by any means possible. He is giving you a charge to guard him and keep him prayerfully. Defend him against the enemy. Be aware that the enemy's strategy is to ruin him through the hands of men who lust for power. He has given him to you as a friend to watch over his life, pray for him, bless him, and stand with him. He wants you to be his friend and brother. You have been brought here for such a time as this. The Lord has brought you here to guard this man's back because the enemy is seeking to destroy him. He wants to kill him because he knows that if he cuts off the head, the body will die. But your friendship is going to be significant throughout the whole region. There are spirits of accusation going out against this man all the time; there is a weakening in the spiritual realm around this man's life. The enemy wants to kill him, to destroy his reputation, because there is a father's heart emerging in him. There is an apostolic calling on his life. The Lord has brought you here to guard his back. Not to be his yes man, but to be his strong right arm."

THE BLESSING OF THE LORD MAKES RICH... As I spoke, John began to cry. The others in the room thought it was because of the incredible privilege God had given him. That may be partly true, but he was also crying because I was speaking to him on one level, and God was speaking to him on a deeper one.

It is not a prophet's job to convict someone of their sin. That's the work of the Holy Spirit and, quite frankly, He doesn't need our help doing it. As I prophesied blessing on John, he was being convicted of his sin at that same moment. He realized that he was on the wrong side of God, and he had been doing the very things the enemy wanted him to do. He was being convicted even as blessing was being poured out on him.

John felt very guilty in that moment, but that's okay. After all, guilt is a friend because it convinces us that we are wrong and need to repent. Guilt is different than condemnation, which makes us feel so bad that we cannot approach God for forgiveness. Guilt, however, leads us back to Christ.

At a time when any human being would have slapped John around for his sin, God gave mercy and grace. "Isn't it time we changed this?" God whispered to him. Even as I prophesied the blessing, God was showing him the root of sin. He was prompting John to change from vicious backstabbing to his true call. Where sin abounds, grace abounds so much more.

In the spirit, I could feel John's resolve strengthen. He determined that he would answer the call of God on his life. "I want to be that man," he prayed, and he has been since that day. His heart broke when God honored him—and he responded.

Almost twenty years later, John and David are best friends. They have held on to each other through good times and bad. Their friendship has been significant regionally, drawing churches together around their ministry. Both guys teach on how to live together and deal with confrontation. Their ministry is superb.

Later that weekend, I took John aside and asked if everything was okay with him.

"You have no idea how God has blessed me this weekend!" he said. At that point, I felt the Lord nudge me to tell him what I had been shown.

"Actually, I think I might," I said. "On Friday night, I saw you with a knife in your hand, stabbing David in the back."

He broke down in tears; a contrite spirit knows the kindness of God. The fact that the Lord knew his sin, but redeemed and blessed him publicly without exposing it, softened his heart.

"You didn't say anything," he said.

...AND ADDS NO SORROW WITH IT

"God had something better to say than that," I said.

"Why did He bless me?" he asked.

I looked him in the eyes. "John," I said, "that's what God is like. He's the kindest person I've ever met in my life. God was only being true to his essential nature. It's impossible for Him to be anything but kind. God is good, and His goodness leads us to repentance."

That is the beauty of the prophetic. Anyone can speak to what is there, but only God can go beyond that and speak to what could come. Why speak to the flesh when you can speak to the treasure? If we do not understand the diagnostic principle, we may prophesy a problem and cause major damage. The Gospel is redemptive: a prophet must be good news, even if that news is repentance.

"*We have this treasure in earthen vessels,*" Paul said (2 Corinthians 4:7). It is better to speak to the treasure rather than just the clay pot. Whatever you speak to in people will rise up. If you speak to nobility, it emerges. If you speak to the Christ-like nature, He is revealed. If we connect with someone's carnality, it will rise up too.

Sometimes, because of our intransigence, the Lord will have to chastise rather than mildly rebuke. This may be more formal and public than we would like. It is our nonresponsiveness that

GOD DOES NOT DO SHAME

has brought this about, and we only have ourselves to blame. But usually, that only comes when we are so far

SAINT JOAN OF ARC

LIVED: 1412 to 1431

PROPHETIC SYNOPSIS: With her country under siege, God visited Joan, a young farm girl in rural France, with a series of prophetic messages. Shortly after her thirteenth birthday, Joan spent a day fasting and praying. During that fast, God spoke to her: "When I was about thirteen, I received revelation from our Lord by a voice which told me to be good and attend church often and that God would help me." From that time on, she heard various voices speak to her, including Michael the Archangel, St. Catherine, and St. Margaret of Antioch. Two or three times a week, Joan would receive a message from one of those famed servants of God.

The voices told her she had to go to end the siege of a town called Orleans, take a young ruler named Charles to a city called Rheims and crown him King of France. It was a call that would change Joan's life.

Five years later, God's voice told her to go to the neighbouring town of Vaucouleurs and speak to the captain of the fortress there, a man named Robert de Baudricourt. She immediately recognized Robert, even before he was introduced to her. Joan kept telling Robert that she had to meet Charles the Dauphin; he refused her twice. Finally, she prophesied to Robert that the French would win a battle at Herrings. They did, and Robert, impressed, gave Joan six attendants and ordered them to take her to Chinon, where Charles was.

Just as her revelation showed, Joan led the French army to victory and crowned Charles king. Burned at the stake at age nineteen for being a heretic, she died staring at a makeshift cross made by an enemy soldier.

KEY COMMENT: "I fear nothing for God is with me!"

MORE: Read *Joan of Arc* by Mark Twain or *Joan of Arc: In Her Own Words* by Willard Trask.

Sources: Mark Twain. *Joan of Arc: Personal Recollections*, trans. Jean François Alden. (Ignatius Press, 1990). Willard Trask. *Joan of Arc: In Her Own Words*. (New York: Turtle Point Press, 1996).

down the road of no return that He considers it the only way to bring redemption. We don't have to speak the negative, even if God reveals it to us. If we fix in our minds that the Gospel is redemptive, we will be more likely to speak to the treasure God has for people.

If possible, draw attention to the leaders in the church before you give any corrective word (NB. Please see book 2 in the series, entitled *Prophetic Protocol*). At least try to make it as private as possible so as not to cause shame or condemnation.

If you are in a public event such as a conference, and you receive such a word for someone and there is no possibility of a more private meeting with a few people, then care must be taken to extend grace. Give the prophecy as a general "word to someone here" and request that they see you privately. Then it is up to the Holy Spirit to lovingly confront, convict, and redeem!

GRACE BREAKS OUR HEARTS

The grace of God will keep flowing into our lives most of the time. There isn't a person in any church, anywhere, to whom God doesn't want to reveal His incredible kindness. Many Christians have given up on the kindness of God. Our experiences with others have been so bad that we can't help but equate God with natural relationships. But God is completely different: He is not human. He is divine, an altogether different character.

God wants to build us up any way He can. Prophecy is for the edification, comfort, and encouragement of those who receive it. God isn't just encouraging and stirring us — He is in touch with our pain as well. He wants to bring us comfort when we need it.

Ninety percent of prophecy is stating the obvious: God loves you, He cares for you, He wants the best for you, His kindness and faithfulness is with you. His love is eternal. He knows everything about your life. These are things every Christian knows and recites, but sometimes we get so locked into our circumstances that we lose sight of even those basic attributes of the character of God. We need to be reminded from time to time. We can read these same truths in Scripture, but sometimes we just need that "now" element of prophecy, allied to the Bible, to actually bring the word home to our circumstances in a dynamic way.

We must not apologize if the prophecy we have is not new or fresh. If we have received a word that God loves someone, then we have to say that word in the best way possible. Prophecy communicates spirit-to-spirit as well as speaking to our minds.

The whole essence of prophecy is that we need to let the Holy Spirit fire our spirits. Personally, the fact that God loves me is the single most important truth in my life. I know that He loves me.

I wake up every day convinced of the love of God, convinced that something wonderful is going to happen that day between me and the Lord, convinced that God is going to help me find a way through the problems I have in my life at the moment. God is going to do something terrific and dynamic, and He is going to help me fight off the enemy and fight through the difficulties. Why? Because He loves me. It doesn't matter what is facing me in life at the moment, for I know that God is going to walk with me. The worst that can happen is that my situation doesn't change at all, but I know the presence of God. God will walk me through it. I'll have to go through everything and endure everything, but even in that, God will not leave me. His presence will be with me. He will be with me even until the end of the age.

The absolute best that can happen is that He changes everything and my concerns disappear. The worst that can happen is that I get to walk by faith for a little while longer. His presence is with me as I endure, and even the struggle is wonderful.

DISCERNMENT AND DIRECTION

IN CHRIST, EVERYTHING IS WITHIN OUR REACH

My confidence in the love of God colors the way I prophesy. Thank the Lord it does! Sometimes when we pray for a person, we can be given the gift of discerning spirits, along with our prophetic intuition. Primarily, discernment enables us to detect and witness God at work. However, it can also enable us to understand the spiritual state of an individual. There are no secrets from the Holy Spirit: He knows everything about everyone. Discernment can be helpful as it can tell us if an evil spirit is present, if the person is oppressed or possessed, and if they are under some form of spiritual attack.

In prayer times, the Lord has often shown me the spiritual state of the person I am prophesying over. For example, I have detected a profoundly low self-esteem. Of course, the last thing you want to do when praying for someone with low self-esteem is broadcast to a room of five hundred people that they have a poor self-image. We must not prophesy the problem. Instead, we must speak out what God wants to be for them.

"A new confidence is going to come into your life from the Lord," one might pray over a person with low self-esteem. "Through events in your life, God is going to meet you and take you to a whole new level of peace, rest, and confidence. He'll take you to a place you've never been before and you'll love it. As He does that, the Lord says He will break some long-standing things in you. Your life is at the point of breakthrough. A spirit of breakthrough hovers over your life right now and it will enable you to get revenge over the enemy for all the areas where you have felt pushed down over the years." In Isaiah 61, we have the favor of God and the possibility of vengeance on the enemy for all of our situations.

When we exit the prison of our circumstances, we are able to receive the Lord's blessing and turn our life into an opportunity to strike back at the enemy.

Whatever we have suffered and been a victim of in life, now, when freedom comes, it enables us to use our favor to set people free from the very thing we ourselves were a victim of in life. It is a critical part of the prophetic gift to declare God's heart, intention, and favor to another and to proclaim that their own breakthrough will lead them to assist others in overcoming!

By speaking to what God wants to do, and not what the individual, the world, or the enemy has already done, we speak freedom into a person's life. If we see a particular sin over someone's life, it has not been revealed to us so we can pronounce judgment. We need to wait and listen for further insight and instruc- **OUR MATURITY MAY WELL DEPEND ON THE TYPE OF QUESTIONS WE ASK**
tion from above. He shows us sin because there is a release in the Spirit over the person's life. Our question must be: "What is the nature of that release?" God is not heartless. He will not show us sin without showing us the critical point of release that's about to come into that person's life.

Seeing someone's sin prophetically boils down into one question: "Is this a grace issue or a discipline issue?" When we sense something is amiss, we have to dig into our spirit and listen very closely to what God has to say. Does He want grace or discipline? If it is a grace issue, we have to prophesy grace, mercy, and hope.

A few years ago, I remember seeing a spirit of lust sitting on a man I was praying for. It was almost oppressing him, but I felt God telling me that it was a grace issue. God showed me what was going to happen, and I prophesied it: "A new anointing of holiness is coming upon you. I see a fresh anointing for holiness that will bring you to a whole new place of purity, power, and righteousness. You've been crying out for those things and God is delighted to say yes, with all of His heart." Men break open when you prophesy holiness over them: many have been crying out for that new path, and God loves to open it to people.

There are also times when we see a sin and God declares it a discipline issue. This occurs when a person has been ignoring the grace of God for a long time. Pride and arrogance accompany that sin. In Scripture, we see this dealt with a few times. Paul, for example, told the Corinthian church to throw out a man who was having sex with his own mother. It was a deplorable, abhorrent sin and the individual had to be disciplined. We can also be disciplined in a Hebrews 12 context, where God is developing us into mature sons and daughters. *"If you endure chastening, God deals with you as with sons; for what son is there whom a father does not chasten?"* says Hebrews 12:7–8. *"But if you are without chastening, of which all have become partakers, then you are illegitimate and not sons."* Loving confrontation is sometimes required in discipline.

One rule holds true whether it is a grace issue or a discipline issue—you always deal with sin privately, not publicly. In 1986, the elders of a church I was visiting asked me to pray for a man who was going through a very hard time. His wife wouldn't go to church, wouldn't pray with him, and didn't want to talk about Jesus. They asked me to go and encourage him.

DISCIPLINE, WHEN STORED UP BY OUR LACK OF RESPONSE... BECOMES CHASTISEMENT

As I prayed for him, with the elders present, I saw a vivid picture of the man in a navy pinstripe suit, with a white shirt and red striped tie. He was walking into the foyer of the Connaught Hotel with a redheaded woman. The woman was wearing a two-piece, dark green business suit and carried an overnight bag. They went to the reception desk and signed in under the name "Coleman." The attendant, a bald, 5'2" man in a black suit, white shirt, and green tie, gave him a key for room 213.

After seeing that, I asked the Lord what it meant. God told me that his wife was all over the place because the man had been having an affair with his secretary for three years. She knew something was wrong but didn't have any proof. She could not stand his hypocrisy and became depressed.

I had been asked to pray for a man who seemingly had a shrew for a wife; that perception turned out to be all wrong! I asked the Lord one final question: "Is this a grace issue or a discipline issue?"

"I have been speaking to this man for three and a half years, Grae," the Lord said to me. "It's a discipline issue. Tell him what I've shown you."

I shared the vision and watched as the man sunk to his knees, crying. The elders were perplexed: "Who is this woman?" they asked him. "Your wife is a blond! Your name is not Coleman!"

The man confessed everything: on business trips, the two would stay at the Connaught Hotel, and the last time they were there, they had room 213.

This man was at the point of losing everything because he had resisted God's grace for three and a half years. We had reached a point of critical mass and God had to deal with the issue. The man could not be trusted to respond to a grace word any longer; he had to be lovingly confronted and led to a place of confession and repentance.

When we encounter a discipline issue, we must remember that the whole point God has brought it up is to lead the individual into confession and repentance. Paul's exhortation in Galatians 6:1 must be of paramount concern to us: *"Brethren, if a man is overtaken in any trespass, you who are spiritual restore such a one in a spirit of gentleness, considering yourself lest you also be tempted."* Judging someone will not cause them to change. Restoring them in gentleness will.

Any time someone receives a prophetic word, grace should explode in their hearts. If someone is walking in sin, they usually don't need to be told about it because they already know. We don't need to be prophesying what a person's problem is, we need to be prophesying what God wants to do at that moment in time.

I once did a conference with a team of prophetic people in the northeastern United States. We were praying during a ministry time when I came to a natural break in what I was doing. I stood back for a moment to gather myself in the spirit and found myself listening to what another speaker was prophesying over a young man.

"The Lord sees you as a very hard nut with a very hard exterior," he told the man. "In the next twelve months, God is going to crack open your life." In graphic detail, this man prophesied the pain and pressure God was going to pour out on this poor person's life, all to crack him wide open. I was getting depressed just listening to it—I can't imagine what the poor man was feeling!

"I don't like this," I said to the Lord. My heart was jarred by the words this man had given. This person had nothing to look forward to for the next twelve months; it was like his life was going to be flushed down a toilet for a whole year. The man finished

ALWAYS ASK: WHAT IS THE FREEDOM AND THE RELEASE?

prophesying and walked away, leaving a devastated young Christian in his wake. He didn't know what to do or where to look. He was totally lost.

I walked over to him and put my hand on his shoulder. He flinched.

"It's okay, mate," I said.

"Please, I don't want another prophecy," he replied. I'm not surprised, I thought to myself.

"Okay," I said. "Why don't you and I just be two guys, two brothers, on a journey together? We're both on a quest with God, so let's just see what else He might have to say."

I asked the Lord to show me the first thing He had shown the other man. God showed me a very hard nut, one that could be pounded on a table but make no sound. It was rock hard. "Okay, Lord," I prayed. "Was there anything else you wanted to show him, something he didn't get?" Suddenly, right next to the nut in my picture was a bottle of oil.

The first prophetic person had gone with the first thing he had seen. He didn't wait or dig deeper into what God wanted to do. He didn't ask any questions. God had given him the nut picture as information to contextualize the actual word.

"What's with this nut?" I asked God. The Lord showed me that the man had lived a hard life. He wasn't rebellious or hard-hearted; life had just been difficult. He had to build a shell around him to protect himself from all the damaging things he had grown up with. He was an orphan. He lived in institutions but was never chosen for a home. He never got adopted. He never received anything. He had known all kinds of abuse. That hard shell was the only way he could have kept himself together. God showed me he was a nice kid. He had come to the front because he desperately wanted God.

God doesn't break nuts by shattering them. When I asked Him how He wanted to break this hard shell, I saw a picture of the oil bottle being opened and poured on to the nut. It didn't happen just once; it happened again, and again, and again, and again. The mysterious ways of God softened that nut to the point that one could dig their fingernails into it and pry it apart. It wasn't hard anymore.

I told the young man that I saw a nut. His face was priceless: "Oh no, it's going to happen again!"

"Next to the nut, I see a big bottle, full of oil," I continued. "I see it being poured on to that nut, again, and again, and again. It is a continuous stream of activity, oil being poured out so lavishly that the nut suddenly became soft. I believe that all of your experiences of life to date have made you tough and hard on the outside. God knows everything you have gone through just to preserve your own life. And now He is saying, 'My son, My son, the days of hardness are over. These are the days of a softening, a day when the oil of My presence and beauty will soften you.' The Lord says that the next season will be a profound season of change — a transformation. You will dance your way through this time, you're going to laugh your way through this time, you're going to grin your way through this time, you're going to smile your way through this time, for the days of hardness are at an end. These are days of a continuous grace and an oil of the Holy Spirit being poured out on you. Enjoy this time."

Something in his heart began to connect with God when I prayed for him. A few minutes later, I saw him on his knees, worshiping. He was changed by that word.

PEACE, NOT PRESSURE

One of my good friends often jokes that prophecy is eighty percent preparation, twenty percent inspiration, a hundred percent perspiration, and a thousand percent trepidation. Often, the main cause of failure in the prophetic is that we have moved under pressure rather than in peace and relaxation in the knowledge of God. I am under enormous pressure, everywhere I go, to move in prophecy. I have visited churches where leaders have slept in sleeping bags outside of my bedroom, wanting a prophetic word in the middle of the night. I've gone to the washroom at 3 a.m. and been followed in by a person wanting prophecy. I have been at conferences where I have been expected to prophesy from 6 a.m. at a men's breakfast straight through to when I wrap up the main session at 11 p.m.

I accept some pressure as part of my ministry, but there is no way I can live under the weight of false or unfair expectations. Many churches and leaders see prophetic ministry as a glorious shortcut. Instead of laboring to create vision in the church from the roots up,

PROPHECY INVOLVES A LABOR OF LOVE AND A WORK OF GRACE

leaders bring in a prophet to prophesy a vision that can be imposed on the people from the top down.

Prophecy will confirm and broaden a vision, it can be a catalyst in the Spirit to reveal the unseen and unknown. Vision is further developed through prayer, seeking God, and sharing our hearts and dreams with people in the work.

Every day, I have to push away the burdens of other people's expectations. To be still, to live in the grace of God, to be aware of His presence, and to be at rest are the goals of prophetic ministry. Into that environment, God can drop His word, create faith, and release the prophetic flow. Worship is important to a prophet. Being at rest and peace in our relationship with God is absolutely vital.

When we do not dwell in rest and peace, we find ourselves reacting to situations. Reaction, rather than rest, is poison for a prophet. People moving under pressure can often indulge in mental gymnastics rather than hearing a word in their spirits. Prophecy becomes tainted.

Most people think prophecy comes from "somewhere out there" into our minds. This isn't the case. In fact, we cannot receive prophecy in our minds. The mind only receives information. Our spirit, however, receives revelation. Prophecy comes from within, through our spirit's communion with the Holy Spirit. It then moves from our spirit into our mind, through the link of faith. Faith is the vehicle that takes a prophetic word from our spirit into our conscious mind.

Our minds are very good at putting things in order. They can organize billions of gigabytes of information, sorting it and making it understandable. Revelation comes in bits and pieces sometimes. We may receive part four, then part two, followed by parts one and three. The mind is brilliant at putting those pieces into order so that they come out correctly. We must always let our faith loose on a prophetic word first, so that it can move from our spirits into our minds. This faith is simply the confidence that the word we have is truly from the Lord.

Sometimes we can get a word coming into our spirits that makes no sense whatsoever to our minds. That is because our minds cannot understand revelation; they can only process it and put it in order. Revelation, sometimes, is totally illogical. It does not always make reasonable sense. If we seek to understand revelation with our minds, we can slip into uncertainty and fear, and become paralyzed by the thought of being wrong. Our courage can evaporate as we ponder the very real possibility of looking stupid in front of other people. That fear can cause someone to cut their losses and say nothing. To make up for it, we often say something general (but dressed up in spiritual language) that our mind can cope with, rather than the significant, supernatural word we've been given.

In a meeting in London several years ago, I gave an appeal for people who were experiencing relational difficulties to come forward for prayer. As I worked through the line, I came to man in his late forties. I had no idea about the relationship in his life that was causing him pain; the man said nothing to me. All I could do was reach out in my spirit and ask God's perspective.

At that instant, I had a fifty-fifty chance at being right about speaking out whether it was a male or female this individual was having trouble with. If I guessed correctly there, the odds lengthened, as I had to decide if it was a mother, wife, girlfriend, sister, daughter, employer, co-worker, church member, pastor's wife, or a hundred other relational possibilities.

As I reached out to God, I said, "The Lord wants to speak to you about your wife." At that point, I received a picture of a tall young woman in her mid- to late-twenties with long blond hair. My mind was screaming at me that this was his daughter. However, in my spirit, I heard the word "wife."

ALL PROPHECY FLOWS FROM INTIMACY

I took a second to rest in my spirit and let my faith loose on the original word. I ignored my mind and spoke prophetically. The word spoke of how the man had been married for three years to a woman twenty years his junior. Under his love and care, she had blossomed in her personality and had changed considerably. She had grown from a mousy introvert into a more confident and outgoing personality. This had changed the dynamic of their relationship to a point where he was becoming less confident of her love and more convinced that she would leave him for a younger man. Into that situation, the Lord spoke a beautiful word of comfort and reassurance that lifted his spirit immeasurably.

Very often, a real battle is waged within our life between our mind and our spirit. Our mind wants to be in control, but God has created our spirit to know Him and move with Him. This is why peace, quiet, and rest on the inside are so vital to a healthy spiritual life.

Some people are "feelers" in the prophetic. We feel people's pain, joy, excitement, or other emotion. We feel things from the heart of God. Some people are "seers." We see in pictures and have dreams. We live a life of metaphor and symbolism. Some people are "hearers." Sometimes, we can move in all three. It is a good thing not to get locked into one methodology. Try to have a variety of ways to receive and deliver prophetic words. After all, God Himself is full of infinite variety.

DEAL WITH FRUSTRATION

Frustration can be an enemy—or an ally—of any prophetic ministry. If left unchecked, it colors our thinking, infects the word we have, and gives us a jaundiced perspective on the life of the Church. If we are to represent God's heart and be good servants, we must learn to master our frustration. We need the understanding and the grace of God to move our hearts rather than our own irritation and dissatisfaction.

As dangerous as frustration is, it can also be incredibly fruitful. I'm not afraid of frustration because it is a vital part of a person's spiritual development. How we handle our and others' frustration is important. Every one of us must handle our frustration wisely and righteously. We cannot shoot our mouth off and blurt out any thought that comes into our head. Instead, we must let frustration develop us. We may be frustrated with our ministry, but often God is in that frustration, trying to change the way we live.

FRUSTRATION IS A SURE SIGN THAT YOU NEED TO CHANGE!

Frustration has a cutting edge, like a double-edged sword. It is okay for us to be frustrated with where our church is, with what the vision is, with the number of meetings, and the rest of the complaints one hears regularly in church life. But we must recognize that there is the other edge to frustration: when we feel frustrated, it's probably because God is frustrated with where we are in our character. God is exceedingly direct. We feel frustrated, and then He reveals its source—a stagnant prayer life, a lack of worship, a decrease in love, a habitual sin. We want to talk about our frustration, but He wants to deal with the one we're causing Him. The Holy Spirit will speak to us in the midst of frustration about our personal walk with God.

MARTIN LUTHER

LIVED: 1483 to 1546

PROPHETIC SYNOPSIS: The man who changed Church history forever spent hours meditating on a particular piece of Scripture. It is clear from his own words that God spoke to him through it:

"As I meditated day and night on the words 'as it is written, the righteous person shall live by faith,' I began to understand that the righteous person lives by the gift of a passive righteousness, by which the merciful God justifies us by faith. This immediately made me feel as though I had been born again, and as though I had entered through open gates into paradise itself. God accepts Christ's righteousness, which is alien to our nature, as our own. Though God does not actually remove our sins—we are at the same time righteous and sinful—he no longer counts our sins against us. And now, where I had once hated the phrase, 'the righteousness of God,' I began to love and extol it as the sweetest of phrases, so that this passage in Paul became the very gate of paradise to me."

Saddened by the state of the faith and Church leadership, Luther nailed ninety-five theses on to the door of a church in Wittenberg, sparking the Reformation and the creation of the Protestant Church.

KEY COMMENT: "The Church does not need any head other than Christ because it is a spiritual body, not a temporal one."

MORE: Read *By Faith Alone* by Martin Luther

Source: Martin Luther. *By Faith Alone.* (Tulsa Oklahoma: World Publishing, 1998).

At least frustrated people care about something. I would rather teach in a room of fifty frustrated people than five hundred apathetic ones.

Rejection is an issue that often walks hand-in-hand with frustration. When we feel rejected, we must open our hearts so that the love of God can flow in. Many prophetic people can feel rejected because they do not have any relationships of worth or value. Prophets are often accused of being weird, temperamental, emotional, and abnormal. In some places where there is a great ignorance of the role of the prophet, that type of behavior is seen as normal for prophetic people. This is a bit of an unfair reputation, as prophets have not cornered the market

YOUR APATHY IS THE GOAL OF THE ENEMY

in abnormality; there are many non-prophetic ministries that seem to fluctuate between the oddball and the highly entertaining.

Prophecy is about restoring people's dignity and self-respect — to do so, we have to be restored ourselves. I hate the enemy because he strips that away from people. He steals dignity and self-respect and creates a sense of disillusionment in our hearts about ourselves. He creates a sense of "I'm not worthy, I'm no good, I can't do anything." He steals every shred of self-worth he can.

Perhaps no more obvious example of this exists than in the world of advertising. Looking spiritually at the ad industry leads me to believe it borders on the demonic a lot of the time, because it is geared to making people feel dissatisfied with their lives. That's the whole point of it: advertisers have to make people unhappy with an aspect of their lives, and if they can achieve that, there is a good chance that people will buy their products. Advertisers create dissatisfaction about our lifestyles, our figures, our looks, our clothes, our possessions, and countless other things. Into that vacuum, they put their own product, hoping to entice us to purchase it and fill the void that they created in the first place. They trade on our insecurities and our need to be loved and valued.

The enemy's strategy works on that same principle. He is geared to making us feel dissatisfied with who we are. He wants to separate us from God, the Church, our friends, and any useful function we may adopt in furthering the Kingdom. If he can get us to hate ourselves and tell our hearts that we are of no account and, as such, it doesn't matter if we don't go to the meeting or pray or worship, then apathy will follow. If we allow apathy into our lives, then it will hold the door open to unbelief, condemnation, self-loathing, bitterness, anxiety, fear, misery, and selfishness. All these things spell passivity, a passive acceptance of life and a demoralized outlook on the things of God. The prophetic is geared to challenging this whole issue, as it is based in the truth of God's love, grace, kindness, and mercy.

EYES OF THE SPIRIT... NOT THE FLESH

Frustration can easily move us into "prophesying" what we see or understand in the natural. A lot of prophetic people make the mistake of looking for clues from people, trying to pick something up from how someone looks (*i.e.* happy or sad), body language, or other traits.

This is a very soulish act and produces "prophecy" on a soulish level. If we are going to move out in prophecy, God is the one person we have to be looking at and listening to. We must not try to pick up clues from people or circumstances. It never works and usually goes wrong. It leads us into the realm of the soul—the mind, will, and emotions—where we can give Satan the opportunity to add to what is going on. What we get may sound spiritual, but it is information, not revelation.

Even the greatest Biblical prophets had to learn this lesson. In 1 Samuel 16:6–13, we read of how Samuel had to reject all physical and cultural clues before he could anoint the next king of Israel:

When they entered, he looked at Eliab and thought, "Surely the Lord's anointed is before Him." But the Lord said to Samuel, "Do not look at his appearance or at the height of his stature, because I have rejected him; for God sees not as man sees, for man looks at the outward appearance, but the Lord looks at the heart."

Then Jesse called Abinadab and made him pass before Samuel. And he said, "The Lord has not chosen this one either." Next Jesse made Shammah pass by. And he said, "The Lord has not chosen this one either." Thus Jesse made seven of his sons pass before Samuel. But Samuel said to Jesse, "The Lord has not chosen these." And Samuel said to Jesse, "Are these all the children?" And he said, "There remains yet the youngest, and behold, he is tending the sheep." Then Samuel said to Jesse, "Send and bring him; for we will not sit down until he comes here." So he sent and brought him in.

Now he was ruddy, with beautiful eyes and a handsome appearance. And the Lord said, "Arise, anoint him; for this is he." Then Samuel took the horn of oil and anointed him in the midst of his brothers; and the Spirit of the Lord came mightily upon David from that day forward. And Samuel arose and went to Ramah.

In a Middle Eastern culture like Israel, all family rights belonged to the oldest son. Obviously, Eliab was a strong, handsome young man with some level of authority, as Samuel immediately thought he was called to be king. But God wanted Samuel to look beyond the physical world and see into the hearts of these young men. God knew which brother had a heart like His, and which one would be able to stand the trials and tribulations to come.

TO HEAR PROPERLY WE MUST BE INTIMATE WITH GOD'S HEART

Ignoring physical clues takes an incredible amount of spiritual discipline. At a meeting once, I gave an appeal for ministry that drew a large response. As I watched people come forward, I noticed an elderly man on crutches, a young, green-haired man with zippers and safety pins everywhere, and a stunningly attractive woman all come to the front.

Eventually, after an hour of ministry, I found myself in front of the attractive woman whom I had noticed earlier. I asked her name and she replied in a very throaty voice. I stepped back into my spirit to hear the Lord and was stunned at His words: "Tell him I am not happy." We cannot mishear God in our spirit, but I could hardly believe this word. I asked the Lord what He meant, being conscious that my mind was sending out alarm signals of distress (which it usually does when I receive this kind of revelation).

"Son," the Lord spoke again, "his name is Richard, and I want you to tell him I know his name and that he must change."

I took a deep breath and looked at this person. There was no way to be sure; all the clues said she was female. I had to make a choice. I decided to live in my spirit. I brought a measure of peace to my mind, which was begging me not to do anything stupid. Fear and embarrassment harassed me in those few seconds, but I had to over-come them.

"Richard, God knows your real name and He is not happy with your lifestyle," I said. "You have to change."

Before I could add a word more, Richard let loose with a string of obscenities, hiked up his long skirt, and ran from the building—closely followed by several other females. No one knew who they were, and to my knowledge, they have not been seen since. Still, I periodically pray that God would complete His work in the life of a transvestite named Sylvia or Richard.

Relying on clues just isn't an option for those who want to prophesy maturely. In a U.S. meeting once, the Lord gave me a word for a man at the rear of the auditorium. He was dressed like a vagrant, an absolute down-and-out character.

God began to give me a word that this man would have hundreds of thousands of dollars to sow into the church, that through his work he was going to lead key businesspeople to the Lord, and that he would finance various projects in the community and the nation. I looked hard at him—he looked like he needed a hand-out. Adding to my dilemma was the fact that right behind him sat a man in a business suit, looking like a million dollars. The individual behind the vagrant looked like he was the executive of a multinational corporation.

I mulled it over in my spirit. My first instinct had been to give the word to what looked like the poorer man, but the clues screamed a different story. Had I mixed the two up? I couldn't get any peace about it, so I wandered away and gave a few words to others in the congregation. I came back to the vagrant and the businessman.

I'm going to have to go for it, I thought to myself. *Ignore the clues and trust the Spirit.* Sometimes, prophecy is just about being brave and launching out. I asked the vagrant to stand up and started prophesying to him. No one in the room seemed to know him, and I was convinced the whole crowd was thinking the same thing: "He's missed it. It's the guy behind him." The man wasn't giving me any help whatsoever; he stared at me, stony-faced. There wasn't a flicker of emotion or recognition to be had.

Some people don't give us any help, often because they don't know how to behave. They have never received a prophetic word before. They don't quite know what to do with themselves, and they are as embarrassed as we are. Sometimes people's faces are very mobile, and they give us a lot of help and encouragement, building our confidence. At other times, people are really trying to "psych out" the prophet. A word can be absolutely on target, but you would never know it by looking at the face of the recipient. I have even prophesied over people who have stared back at me with an insolent, "let's see how good you are" look on their faces. Prophets cannot trust people's faces for confirmation. Our own peace and rest in the Lord should be sufficient encouragement.

YOUR HUMILITY WILL DE-STRESS YOU AND... I prophesied over the vagrant and discovered later on that he was an extremely wealthy individual who liked dressing down. He had heard about the conference and decided to check it out. After I had given him the word, he sat down and I carried on with the meeting.

A few minutes later, I received a word for the man in the suit behind the vagrant. "The job you have just interviewed for is yours," I heard in my spirit. This added to my unsure feelings. On the surface, it seemed that the wealth word was for the suit, and the job word was for the vagrant.

As you can imagine, the enemy was stirring up as much confusion in me as possible. Everything on the inside of me was screaming, "You fool! You idiot! You've got it wrong!" I tried to look cool on the platform, but I was full of anxiety in my soul.

I could do only one thing: humble myself before God. "Lord," I prayed silently, "I will face this situation honorably if I have missed it; I will repent and put things right with people. I will publicly apologize and make sure no one is damaged by any mistake I have made."

The enemy hates humility because he cannot penetrate it. Humility opens a door for God to touch our lives. As I quietly humbled myself on the platform, I experienced a peace and rest in the Lord. I gave the man in the suit his word, and watched with gladness as he and his family punched the air with delight. Later, I learned that he had been unemployed for two years and had been to his first job interview in months that afternoon. A week later, he was offered the job.

I was relieved and very grateful to the Lord. Prophetic ministry is never straightforward. It is ridiculously easy to make mistakes even after years of practice. People apply impossible standards to the prophetic office that they don't assign to any other ministry. I believe that if we relaxed the standards and allowed for more grace, we would actually have fewer prophetic mistakes and a lot more honesty and integrity in the gifting. Pressure is a great enemy of prophets: we are under immense pressure to perform and be super-spiritual. Christians sensationalize the gifting and create a hype and mystique around personalities that is, frankly, immoral and dangerous. We are called to be ourselves in the Lord, within our scope of function.

I do not have to be under pressure to be prophetic. I have to be myself in Jesus, and people can either cope with that or not. It is almost inevitable that we will thrill some people and disappoint others, depending on what is happening when we go to particular places.

...DISTRESS YOUR OPPOSITION

Prophets must never move out in what they see naturally. We cannot lean on our own understanding. Instead, we have to draw out what God has already put in place.

Sometimes, prophetic ministry stands with one foot in the past and the other in the future. We bring both of those extremes into the present to help people make sense of where they are right now.

In 1 Samuel 1:12–18 we see how easy it is for a prophet to get something wrong.

> *Now it came about, as she continued praying before the Lord, that Eli was watching her mouth. As for Hannah, she was speaking in her heart, only her lips were moving, but her voice was not heard. So Eli thought she was drunk. Then Eli said to her, "How long will you make yourself drunk? Put away your wine from you." But Hannah replied, "No, my lord, I am a woman oppressed in spirit; I have drunk neither wine nor strong drink, but I have poured out my soul before the Lord. Do not consider your maidservant as a worthless woman, for I have spoken until now out of my great concern and provocation."*
>
> *Then Eli answered and said, "Go in peace; and may the God of Israel grant your petition that you have asked of Him." She said, "Let your maidservant find favor in your sight." So the woman went her way and ate, and her face was no longer sad.*

Eli was not practicing his sensitivity to God, he was looking for clues. Hannah was sad and desperate. Her heart was broken. She was probably swaying in her grief and moaning in spirit. I know how that feels!

She was also passionately interceding before God along the lines of her vow. Eli heard none of that. He looked in the natural and then made a judgment on what he thought was her behavior. He thought she was drunk! It is so vital, beloved, that we take our thoughts to a place of captivity in Christ-likeness.

We are destroying speculations and every lofty thing raised up against the knowledge of God, and we are taking every thought captive to the obedience of Christ, and we are ready to punish all disobedience, whenever your obedience is complete. You are looking at things as they are outwardly. If anyone is confident in himself that he is Christ's, let him consider this again within himself, that just as he is Christ's, so also are we. (2 Corinthians 10:5–7)

We prophesy out of our own vision, understanding, and testimony of God. What we think about Him is the most important thing in the world (Revelation 19:10).

RESPONSE TO PROPHECY

Ignoring physical clues is not an excuse to throw out any concern for the person for whom we are prophesying. We must be sensitive and carefully consider the person receiving ministry. When we prophesy over people, we must learn to put margins into the word. Do not be anxious to gush out everything you have received; it is easier to add than to retract. We must not be so eager to prophesy that we fail to consider the needs of the recipient.

If we prophesy over an individual for even a few brief moments, we may speak several hundred words. What is this person doing while we are speaking? He or she is probably standing there in memory mode, frantically trying to remember every single sentence and phrase. Their memory will be selective — it will choose to remember the words that have an immediate application to his or her current circumstances. Only a small percentage will be retained; the rest will be deleted or distorted. The main part of the word could be about the future, but that may be lost. Later on, the individual may panic, trying to remember. The enemy can even try to convince them that the forgotten pieces were the most important part of the prophecy. A sense of disappointment may settle on the receiver.

ALL PROPHETS NEED TO ACT LIKE A SHEPHERD

Even worse, a person may remember the bulk of the words but retain little or nothing of the spirit behind them. Prophecy communicates spirit-to-spirit as well as speaking to our minds. There is a spirit to prophecy that sets it above all other communications. Prophecy I received decades ago still has a spiritual impact on me. The spirit is eternal, and we can still hear the spirit language of the Lord down through the years. We can read the written transcript of a prophecy a thousand times, but if the Holy Spirit touched our spirits at the point of delivery, our hearts will retain the freshness and power of the original word as if it was just given.

If we are going to prophesy into people's lives, we need to be responsible. We need to either bring a tape recorder or notebook to capture the detail of the word and allow people to fully engage with it. A relaxed recipient is more likely to receive communication spirit-to-spirit, which is the goal of all prophecy. The individual can have the words recorded for later, but it's the actual spirit of what God is saying that will live with him or her and change their life.

This is one reason why I don't endorse "private" prophecy. While I do believe in "personal" prophecy — that is, a word individuals receive that is directly for their lives and circumstances — private prophecy is a distasteful practice. My American friends call it "parking lot prophecy," and it occurs outside the constraint of meetings or accountability. It lacks integrity and submission to leadership.

We must earn the right to minister into people's lives. If we are living in a godly fashion and are seeking to behave responsibly, we have nothing to fear from accountability. People must be protected, which is the role of a shepherd. It's important that people hear, understand, and can respond to what God wants them to do and say.

RECORDING PROPHECY

Recording prophecy is an important discipline to get into. A large percentage of Scripture is recorded prophecy, written down as it was delivered. The priesthood had secretaries, the army had recorders who faithfully wrote accounts of orders and battles, and kings and prophets had scribes working with them as normal practice. The New Testament continued that tradition, as evidenced by the entire book of Revelation and the many prophetic insights recorded in the gospels, Acts, and epistles.

Isaiah was told on several occasions to write things on a tablet and a scroll. For example:

Moreover the LORD said to me, "Take a large scroll, and write on it with a man's pen concerning Maher-Shalal-Hash-Baz." (Isaiah 8:1)

Now go, write it before them on a tablet, and note it on a scroll, that it may be for time to come, forever and ever. (Isaiah 30:8)

Jeremiah had an assistant named Baruch help him record all of his prophetic words to Israel and Judah (Jeremiah 36). These records played an important role decades later as the prophet Daniel meditated on them.

Scribes are everywhere in Scripture. Ezra was a gifted scribe, so recognized by the secular king Artaxerxes (Ezra 7) and by the godly leader Nehemiah (Nehemiah 8): *"Ezra the priest, the scribe, expert in the words of the commandments of the LORD, and of His statutes to Israel"* (Ezra 7:11). 1 Chronicles 27:32 notes that King David's scribe was his uncle Jehonathan, *"a counselor, a wise man, and a scribe."* In Exodus 34, God told Moses to write down the *"tenor"* of the covenant between Him and His people.

I carry a portable tape recorder and a supply of tapes wherever I go. I also have written thousands of pages in my journals. If a recording is not practical when I am praying for someone, I will insist that a third person be present to record the word and act as a witness. This not only increases accountability, but it allows the receiver to relax and engage God's Spirit in the word.

If you are not presently journaling the insights you are receiving from God, I strongly encourage you to begin to do so. This self-discipline shows that you are serious in taking care of God's words. It places a high value on them, communicating to the Spirit that you are listening carefully. It also enables you to further develop the revelation, as God can and will illuminate new pieces of it.

Journals do not have to be an elaborate or expensive exercise. Any type of book, format, and process is workable, as long as you commit to keeping it up. Some scribble, others type their thoughts. Some draw, others write poems. The form is unimportant: it is the content that matters. When God speaks to you about something, write it down. When He shows you a picture or highlights a Scripture, record it.

Weeks, months, and even years later, you will be encouraged to see how far God has taken you in the spirit, and how many things He has shared with you that have come to pass.

CONCLUSION

We are all on a journey into the heart of God, and it is a trip that should be enjoyed. We should love the way God speaks to us, and love the way He speaks to others. There is nothing like giving a gracious word that opens another human being to suddenly seeing God for themselves in a new, or improved, way. Having a burden for people is about sharing God's burden for them.

Some days, we will have words of incredible power and rich significance, and we'll think: this is what it's like to really prophesy. On other days, we'll wonder if we can even spell the word prophecy! Some days, we'll get bizarre and outrageous things that we will have absolute faith for. Other days, we'll get similarly "out there" things that we just won't have the faith to buy into. Our confidence will have wavered.

The gift of prophecy doesn't change, but our level of faith does. Some days, our faith is present in huge proportions, and other days, it is the size of a mustard seed.

I was once on an airplane with an individual who was absolutely disparaging Christianity. He essentially told me that it was stupid to be a Christian. He spoke so loudly to me that the entire plane could hear him. My flesh just wanted to slap him, but I tried to retreat into my spirit instead.

"God," I prayed, "give me something to shut him up." The man blathered on: religion is a crutch, there is no God, there is no supernatural. "Give me something, Lord," I prayed. "Show me something."

All the Lord showed me was a picture of a small dog with three legs. It was a Jack Russell terrier, white, except for a black ear. Its name was simply Jack.

"Oh no," I groaned in my spirit. "Give me something better than that."

As he railed on about Christianity, I prayed for him. Finally he stopped and I attempted to strike up a more normal conversation. Eventually I steered the conversation around to his life... job, family, and finally pets.

"What's your favorite animal?" I asked. "Horses, cats, dogs?"

"Oh, I like dogs very much" he said.

PROPHECY IS AN ADVENTURE AND ALL ADVENTURES HAVE RISK

"Do you like big dogs or small dogs?" I asked.

"I hate big dogs, but I like small dogs."

"Like a Jack Russell?" I inquired.

"Yeah," he said.

With each question, I was building my faith in the word God had given me. He likes small dogs, he likes Jack Russell terriers—I decided to just launch the word and go for broke.

"When you were six years old, you had a Jack Russell terrier named Jack," I said. "It was totally white, except for one ear that was completely black. When you were six, the dog was involved in a traffic accident and it had its left, hind leg torn off. When you got the dog to the veterinarian, you prayed in that waiting room. You said, 'Dear God, if You save Jack, I will serve You.'"

We looked at each other as tears streamed down his face.

"James, please don't tell me God doesn't exist," I said. "The same God who saved your dog has been looking out for you, and maybe right now is your chance to meet up with who He is."

On days where our faith isn't present, we need to ask questions. Every question we ask builds up a little more faith until we can go for it all. The Holy Spirit loves questions; we just have to be creative asking them. On the days when our faith is diminished, we can still dialogue with Him. The Holy Spirit isn't bothered by a little faith because He knows that just a mustard seed is enough to move mountains. A joy comes when we start small in faith and grow into fullness. I had little faith when I received that picture of Jack, but it grew as I asked a few questions.

If God allows life to be tough on us on certain days, it's for a reason. He wants to develop our gift and teach us how to be confident in Him.

The Exercise of Prophecy

REFLECTIONS, EXERCISES, AND ASSIGNMENTS

The following exercises are designed with this particular chapter in mind. Please work through them carefully before going on to the next chapter. Take time to reflect on your life journey as well as your prophetic development. Learn to work well with the Holy Spirit and people that God has put around you so that you will grow in grace, humility, and wisdom in the ways of God.

Graham

WHAT CONSTITUTES MATURITY?

Prophetic maturity is concerned with displaying sound wisdom and knowledge alongside good practice and accountable, teachable behavior. It is connected to the development of Christlike characteristics and demonstrating the values and temperament of the Holy Spirit. Within the context of this chapter, you must be willing and able to develop these attributes as a sign of your growing maturity:

- Demonstrate that you understand the life and nature of God for you, and your willingness to behave as Christ would in your current circumstances. Is it clearly evident that you are cultivating a greater perception of God's essential goodness in your own life?

- Pursuing love as a primary source and response in your life. Are you known as someone who models love as a prime value? Actively demonstrating high levels of grace and kindness? Is your personal humility very much to the fore, particularly in difficult situations?

- Regarding your temperament and personality, are you able to exercise the fruit of self-control? Can you prophesy for the common good of the church? A mature person is able to move beyond their own frustration to deliver a clear word from the Lord that edifies the church and produces momentum in difficult circumstances.

- We operate prophetically in a war zone. We live on the battlefield between two kingdoms of light and dark. We will have tribulation and opposition. It is essential that you can demonstrate how to move in the opposite spirit to what comes against you, whether on a spiritual or human level. Do you have a strategy for difficult people? Maturity is treating your grace growers well. It is knowing how to bounce back under attack and demonstrate that everything in life is useful for our growth and development.

- To earn the right to prophesy, you must cultivate a good methodology in using the gift. Maturity in prophecy is the ability to deliver a burden and achieve God's objective even when under pressure in your own life. It is in your capacity to inspire people to move from problem to solution with your encouragement.

- Real maturity lies in answering the following question with your lifestyle and gifting: Can you be trusted? Accountability is always best when provoked from below rather than needing to be imposed from above. Mature people seek out the next level of accountability that is required for the anointing that they desire to move in.

WHAT CONSTITUTES IMMATURITY?

Immaturity develops through a constant failure to learn the lessons of life and spirituality. Bluntly, we are tested on everything we are taught. Grace comforts us when we fail the test; truth prepares our hearts to take it again. When carnality does not decrease, wisdom does not grow, and we are challenged again to put on Christ.

If we are dishonest about what we are learning, we will only react to events and people rather than respond to the Living God. It is one thing to trust the Lord, it is quite another to be trusted by Him! Within the context of this chapter, you must face up to the challenges of ongoing immaturity. Here are the possibilities for your consideration:

- Examine your own heart for signs of unforgiveness, holding grudges, and feelings of bitterness and resentment towards others. How much do you blame others for your own shortcomings? Do you withhold love, acceptance or approval when you don't get your own way?

- When we are present/past in our own relationships, we often manifest rejection. This may lead to us being a loner, who has difficulty building relationships. Our prophesying can be clouded by our personality. How much does your own past influence your present/future relationships?

- A past that has not responded to grace may lead us into a place of being harsh, negative, and judgmental. If our lifestyle is not synchronized with the message of grace, love, and forgiveness, then our prophesying will not reflect the nature of God. Our sense of frustration will challenge the message to be negative, rather than channel us to be positive. Do you habitually see the negative before the positive? Have you developed the anointing to see the second image God is releasing? Is your outlook, temperament and prophetic output more centered in the Old Covenant rather than the New?

- How well are you doing at working through your current issues? Are you defensive when faced with personal truth? Can you be questioned about your lifestyle? To whom are you accountable and do they have the experience and maturity to challenge who you are/are not in the Spirit? The most common form of immaturity is evasive behavior; an unteachable spirit; an independent mindset; and spending all your time with people that you can control or easily dupe.

- Prophesying the problem without a solution is immature and dangerous. Without a sure sense of objective, we cannot give words that release and empower others to improve and go further. When we have not taken issue with our own life, we display a hypocrisy towards others that is rooted in lack of grace. When we are not edifying, we may be pulling someone down. How well do you inspire, encourage, edify, comfort, and empower people with your gift?
- What tests have you passed recently and how has that victory been thoroughly established? What tests have you failed and what impact is that defeat having on your relationship with the Lord, your faith, and your prophesying?

NOTES

WHAT GAME WOULD YOU LIKE TO PLAY
WITH ME?

WHEEL OF FORTUNE

REVEL~~ATIO~~ THE WORDS

L, REVELATION

JESUS IF YOU COULD TAKE ME ANYWHERE
WHERE WOULD IT BE? HIGH CLOUDS/MNTNS.

NOTES

NOTES

NOTES

NOTES

NOTES

NOTES

NOTES

AN ASSIGNMENT

Think of a person around your life at this time, particularly one that you do not know very well.

Read and meditate on Psalm 37:3–5 on their behalf. Ask the Lord to touch your heart with His compassion and intentionality for that person.

Without just quoting the scripture:

1.   How would you encourage this person to trust the Lord and stay in a place of faith?

2.   How does the Lord want them to delight in Him?

3.   Is there a specific desire that God wants to fulfill?

4.   What can you say that would cause them to recommit their heart and trust to God at this time?

5.   Using the scriptures and questions as a guideline, write a card to this person providing specific encouragement into their current life experience of the Father.

NOTES

NOTES

G R A C E   G R O W E R S

We all have difficult people in our lives whom the Lord uses to develop our character, personality, ministry and lifestyle.

1. Identify the people with whom you currently are finding it difficult to love and build a relationship. Make a list. *Boys, Family, People with different beliefs Lindsey, Staley, AJ, people on social media*

2. What is it about these people that you find the most difficult? How do they affect you?
Their ability to spew their opinions, not having common sense about opinion vs fact,

3. What is their perception of you? Is it accurate (even partially)? If so, how? *Not sure, maybe distant*

4. What particular fruit of the Holy Spirit do you need to develop to be with them and to love them effectively? *Kindness*

5. What is God teaching you and changing in you? *Perception*

6. Do the above steps 1–5 for each person on your list.

7. How can you make the first move towards these people?

BY REACHING OUT

NOTES

NOTES

CASE STUDY: MATCHING PROPHETIC DELIVERY WITH CONTENT

The delivery of a prophetic word must match its content. One cannot grab someone by the throat and prophesy love and peace; likewise, a prophecy about warrior strength cannot be properly prophesied in an airy whisper. The context must match the content.

Below are a few prophetic words I have given to individuals enrolled in my prophetic schools (I have changed the names for privacy reasons). In this exercise, read the prophetic word and answer the questions following it.

PROPHETIC WORD

Donna, what I see in the Spirit is you standing under a waterfall. The water is cascading onto your head—the whole waterfall is about the peace and the rest of God. The Lord says He is going to drive out of your brain the capacity to worry, to be anxious, to be fearful, to feel inadequate, to feel insecure, all those things. There is a peace and a rest of God coming to you that is so remarkable, it will change your very personality. In these days, there is a peace so strong, so profound, and so powerful that nothing will be able to make you anxious again. There is a laughter rising up, because the Lord says, "Sweetie, you've cried enough." The Lord says that you were always meant to go through life with a grin. And now He's going to come to you to teach you how to live every day under

His smile. You're going to learn what it is to be precious to God because that's how He sees you. You don't feel precious a lot of the time, but He says to you, "I think you're precious, and because I'm God, what I think matters more than what you think."

The Lord says, "Life is still going to be life for you. There are still going to be difficulties and ups and downs for you — the difference is going to be on the inside of you." You're not going to be up and down, up and down, up and down. The Lord is going to give you a straight, even road to walk on. It's called peace. The Lord says that it's in His heart for you to become one of the most peaceful people of your generation. This rest and peace will bring you to a place of favor with God where you're going to get revenge on the enemy for everything he's ever done to you. Your peace is going to reach out and heal people because a prophetic anointing is going to grow in your heart with a confidence and a certainty. Around you will be a peace, and within you will come a peace. Pressure will come from the outside, but the Lord says that peace will be an equalizing pressure on the inside. He is going to drive out of your head the capacity to worry, to be anxious, to be afraid.

You're standing under a waterfall of peace. So everything inside you is heading into a place of peace, serenity, tranquility, and calm. This is your journey in these days, and the Lord says, "From this moment, every situation you encounter will have peace with it." He will teach you how to access that peace — and when you do that on a regular basis, confidence is going to come, faith is going to come, and then the prophetic is going to rise up inside of you.

ANSWER THE FOLLOWING QUESTIONS:

1. What is the crux (focus) of this word?

    PEACE ; How God plans to Change Her LIFE

2. What is the emotion and plan God has for Donna?

    LIFE CHANGE

3. What would be the best way to deliver this word? What tone of voice would be best to use? What body language and position should be used?   *CALMNESS   STANDING   WITH CONFIDENCE*

4. After delivering the word, what would you pray over her?

    PRAY FOR HER TO BELIEVE AND HAVE FAITH IN THE PLAN.

When peace is the objective, we have to embody it. In my ministry, I love prophesying peace, because I end up feeling just as peaceful as the thing I'm seeing. I can't let something like peace flow out of me without it actually coming in and touching me. It's like a prophetic aftertaste; there's always a bit that flows back into the prophet's own life. When we prophesy in peace, we have to say it in such a way that everything—the way we speak, the way we stand, the way we look—has to flow towards that objective.

NOTES

NOTES

NOTES

NOTES

NOTES

NOTES

NOTES

LECTIO DIVINA

Lectio Divina (Latin for *divine reading*) is an ancient way of reading the Bible—allowing a quiet and contemplative way of coming to God's Word. *Lectio Divina* opens the pulse of the Scripture, helping readers dig far deeper into the Word than normally happens in a quick glance-over.

In this exercise, we will look at a portion of Scripture and use a modified *Lectio Divina* technique to engage it. This technique can be used on any piece of Scripture. I highly recommend using it for key Bible passages that the Lord has highlighted for you, and for anything you think might be an inheritance word for your life (see the *Crafted Prayer* interactive journal for more on inheritance words).

Read the Scripture:

If I speak with the tongues of men and of angels, but do not have love, I have become a noisy gong or a clanging cymbal. If I have the gift of prophecy, and know all mysteries and all knowledge; and if I have all faith, so as to remove mountains, but do not have love, I am nothing. And if I give all my possessions to feed the poor, and if I surrender my body to be burned, but do not have love, it profits me nothing.

Love is patient, love is kind and is not jealous; love does not brag and is not arrogant, does not act unbecomingly; it does not seek its own, is not provoked, does not take into account a wrong suffered, does not rejoice in unrighteousness, but rejoices with the truth; bears all things, believes all things, hopes all things, endures all things.

Love never fails; but if there are gifts of prophecy, they will be done away; if there are tongues, they will cease; if there is knowledge, it will be done away. For we know in part and we prophesy in part; but when the perfect comes, the partial will be done away.

When I was a child, I used to speak like a child, think like a child, reason like a child; when I became a man, I did away with childish things. For now we see in a mirror dimly, but then face to face; now I know in part, but then I will know fully just as I also have been fully known.

But now faith, hope, love, abide these three; but the greatest of these is love. (1 Corinthians 13)

1.   Find a place of stillness before God. Embrace His peace. Chase the unhelpful thoughts out of your mind. Calm your body. Breathe slowly. Inhale. Exhale. Inhale. Exhale. Clear yourself of the distractions of life. Whisper the word, "Stillness." Take your time. When you find that rest in the Lord, enjoy it. Worship Him in it. Be with Him there.

2.   Re-read the passage twice. Allow its words to become familiar to you. Investigate Paul's definition of love. What images does it bring

to your spirit? What do you see? Become a part of it. What phrases or words especially resonate with you? Meditate especially on those shreds of revelation. Write those pieces down in your journal.

3.   Read the passage twice again. Like waves crashing onto a shore, let the words of Scripture crash onto your spirit. What excites you? What scares you? What exhilarates you about this revelation of the love of God? What are you discerning? What are you feeling? What are you hearing? Again, write it all down in your journal.

4.   Write the theme of this passage in your journal.

5.   Does this passage rekindle any memories or experiences? Does it remind you of any prophetic words you have given or received? Write those down as well.

6.   What is the Holy Spirit saying to you through this Scripture? Investigate it with Him — picture the two of you walking through it together. Write those words in your journal.

7. Read the passage two final times. Meditate on it. Is there something God wants you to do? Is there something He is calling you to? Write it down.

8. Pray silently. Tell God what this passage is saying to you. Tell Him what you are thinking about. Write down your conversation together. Picture yourself and the Holy Spirit as two old friends in a coffee shop, chatting about what God is doing.

9. Finally, pray and thank God for His relationship with you. Come back to the passage once a week for the next three months. Read it and let more revelation flow into you. If you feel compelled to, craft a prayer based on this passage for yourself, your family, your friends, or your church. Pray that prayer until you feel God has birthed it in you.

NOTES

NOTES

NOTES

NOTES

NOTES

NOTES

NOTES

NOTES

Moving From Prayer to Prophecy

I first received this whole workshop in a dream more than 25 years ago. In the dream I saw myself doing this workshop in a conference. When I awoke, I wrote out the workshop verbatim and have not changed it from that day to the present.

Tens of thousands of people have stepped into the prophetic gift with absolute ease using this particular model.

This exercise can be done on your own, with another person, or as part of a group exercise where people split into pairs. (If it's a group exercise, try to get with someone you hardly know.)

You will need: pen, paper, and Bible.

WORKSHOP

SPECIFIC INSTRUCTION:

- Bring yourself/the group to peace and rest. Quietly acknowledge God's presence and relax.
- Take one step at a time and complete as close to the time allotted as possible.

Step One: Find a partner!

- Think about the person you are with.
- Ask the Lord questions about them re: how He sees them.
- Get God's heartbeat for them: How much He loves them, what He wants to be for them.

Imagine you have a bow and arrow and that the arrow represents the prayer God is going to give you. Where would you aim this arrow? Into what part of their life would you aim a prayer of blessing and encouragement (*e.g.*, Home, finances, health, job, ministry, marriage, relationship with God, etc.)

- Write down the target area (probably the first one you think of is it).

- In the light of your target area being identified, does your prayer need to change and become more specific? Write accordingly.

Allow 4–8 minutes.

Step Two:

- Write out a prayer of blessing, release and encouragement.
- Allow any pictures, visions, or scriptures to come to mind.
- It is helpful to imagine yourself praying for them. Let a prayer rise up in your heart and write down the main points, then amplify it.
- Write between 4–6 sentences in your prayer.

Allow 5–10 minutes.

Step Three:

Recap: Now we have a prayer of blessing and encouragement for a particular area of life.

- Imagine a computer screen… with your prayer on the screen!
- Change the wording from a prayer to a simple prophetic statement by altering some key words and phrases.

EXAMPLE: TURNING A PRAYER INTO A
SIMPLE PROPHETIC STATEMENT

Prayer

Father, I pray that you will bless David and take your relationship with him to a whole new dimension of the Spirit. I pray that you will become his heart's desire.

I ask that he know you and that your love for him will set his heart on fire with a new passion for intimacy and worship. I ask that you will give him a spirit of wisdom and revelation to know you and your ways to a new depth of understanding and experience.

Prophetic Statement

David, you are coming into a season of blessing that will take your relationship with God to a whole new powerful dimension of the Spirit.

You are going to see, know, understand and experience God in intimacy and worship in a way that will set your heart on fire with a burning passion.

There is a spirit of wisdom and revelation that God is pouring out into your heart in this next season that will impact you greatly and will lead you into a deeper place of the Spirit.

This deeper place of the Spirit will become a strategic well of devotion and praise that will touch the hearts of many people with whom you come into contact.

The anointing upon you will empower people to break free of unbelief and poor vision of God to embrace the Lord in a powerful way.

You will have an anointing to awaken people to a new depth of first love experience in the Lord.

It is inevitable that in turning the prayer into a simple prophetic statement that the word will be expanded to some degree.

- Write out your simple prophetic statement of encouragement and blessing. Add whatever you feel is necessary!

Allow 10–15 minutes.

Step Four: Choose who will begin!

The one speaking: Pray for your partner.

- Give the word slowly and clearly.
- Don't rush it! Be humble and considerate.
- Don't mumble. Don't apologize.
- Trust the Lord in what He has given you.

The recipient: Open your heart to receive encouragement.

- Smile! Nod your head, be attentive.
- Enjoy the experience. The worst thing that can happen is that you get a blessing in the wrong area of your life! (If that

happens, ask the Holy Spirit for the right target area and apply the encouragement!)

- Change over so that both people have equal opportunity to speak and receive.
- Pray for one another to seal in the prophecy.
- Exchange papers!!

Allow 10–15 minutes.

If you finish before the allotted time, share what the word meant to you and encourage your partner.

Step Five: Review of the exercise.

- Who enjoyed it?
- Who was a little scared?
- Who received a blessing?
- Who felt that God spoke to them?
- Who felt God speaking through them?
- What did that feel like?

The premise for this workshop is: if you can pray, you can prophesy!

The same faith faculty that reaches out to the Lord for a prayer is identical to the ones we use when moving in prophecy, *i.e.*, care, love, concern, the heart of God, desire to be a blessing, a will to encourage another, a belief in God's goodness, etc.

- Halfway through this workshop, it ceased to be a workshop only and became body ministry.
- God has spoken to you at this time and the word you have is yours to keep and use.

- Meditate on it and expect the blessing.
- You are now an encourager, so keep going! Do this exercise at least twice a week, either with another person or on your own, and write a card to mail to someone else.

What have you learned?

1. To sit quietly in God's presence.

2. To receive His heartbeat for another person.

3. To hear the Lord in prayer.

4. To receive a sense of direction (arrow)… this is a word of knowledge.

5. How to be sensitive to the Holy Spirit.

6. To write a crafted prayer of blessing and encouragement.

7.   How to craft a prophetic word that will edify, encourage or comfort.

8.   How to give a simple prophecy with sensitivity and faith.

9.   How to record prophecy by writing. (The more you practice and become attuned to God's heart, you may want to consider upgrading the recording aspect to buying a handheld recorder and tapes.)

10. How to convey God's love and desire.

11. How to touch a person's life in a personal way from the Lord!

12. How to seal the word in prayer.

Practice makes perfect. If you will continue this exercise over a period of months, your capacity to hear God and receive prophecy will grow in a very powerful way.
Blessings!

Graham

NOTES

NOTES

NOTES

NOTES

NOTES

NOTES

NOTES

NOTES

NOTES

NOTES

NOTES

NOTES

NOTES

A PROPHECY - A DIVINE ACCELERATION

WE ARE IN A SEASON of Divine Acceleration. There is a Quickening Spirit abroad in the earth. The Lord is redeeming time because the days we are living in are becoming progressively more wicked. Time is the currency that our lives are running on, not money. God redeems time by speeding up the process by which we are transformed. I say to you that there is a quickening spirit upon your life, should you choose to accept it.

What you thought would take years, will take months. What you thought would take months, will take weeks. What you thought would take weeks, will take days. What you thought would take days, will take hours and moments. The favor of the Lord is upon you to accelerate your development in these next twelve months. In this Divine Acceleration, the gap between prophecy spoken and prophecy fulfilled will get narrower and narrower. Eventually, the gap will be so small we will see the release of the "Let there be" word from Genesis one: creative words of prophecy that will bring immediate release and empowerment, particularly to situations where the Church is contending with the enemy for breakthrough.

The Lord will give you five years' growth in the next twelve months. BUT!!! You have to learn to run! You must say yes much faster and mean it. You must stick with the process. Acceleration is a paradox. It is not always easy and it is hugely enjoyable.

I believe the Lord would say to you that, "This is how I want you to see the next twelve months: it is indeed a crash course in the Glory of your God. He would say to you, did I not say to you that if you would believe you would see the Glory of God?

These next twelve months, as you progress, as you speed up in the Spirit, I will give you an anointing. I will renew you in the Spirit of your mind. I will open your heart. The eyes of your heart will be enlightened and you will see the hand of God everywhere in your life. You will look and there will be days, says the Lord, when you will look at your life through My eyes and you will see what I see.

Your heart will be overwhelmed with joy, with laughter. There will be a faith that rises up. There are many quick victories that I intend to give you in your personal walk with Me.

Acceleration is vital, Beloved, because you are behind the time of your own development. I will accelerate your capacity to learn faster and become more obedient to the Holy Spirit in your training.

There are steps to take and keys of revelation and power to receive. Life in Me is not about what you can appropriate in events but what you learn of Me in the process of day-to-day life.

Running from one impartation to another will only empower you to blow up, not grow up. Process is the major part of impartion. I work by Encounter and Experience.

If Encounter comes first, you must learn the process of turning it into a lifestyle experience. Process establishes Truth into Relationship. Knowing how to practice turning an Encounter into an abiding life experience is everything!

If experience comes first, it is because I am giving you prochecy, promise and dreams/visions so that you may understand My intention for you.

In Process you learn the business end of studying to demonstrate your willingness to conform to My Will. It is "I who work in you, to will and to do for My good pleasure."

You must prove that you are ready and willing to practice what you are learning. Without this, it will be difficult to hold onto your own identity. Jesus learned obedience by the things that He went through in life.

So I call you now to practice, practice, practice My Presence, My Truth and My Delight in the process of your training.

I call you up to Love the Learning in each life situation. To lean into Me as your Overcomer. I want you to believe who I AM for you in every life issue. All the clues are in the specific scriptures I give you, also in the promises, prophecy and dreams/visions that I bring to you.

It's time to go further, faster. Are you ready?

RECOMMENDED READING

Title	Author	Publisher
Hearing God	Dallas Willard	InterVarsity Press
The Gift of Prophecy	Jack Deere	Vine Books
Surprised by the Voice of God	Jack Deere	Zondervan
Growing in the Prophetic	Mike Bickle	Kingsway
The Seer	James Goll	Destiny Image
Prophetic Etiquette	Michael Sullivant	Creation House
The Prophet's Notebook	Barry Kissel	Kingsway
User Friendly Prophecy	Larry Randolph	Destiny Image
Prophecy in Practice	Jim Paul	Monarch Books
Can You Hear Me?: Tuning in to the God Who Speaks	Brad Jersak	Trafford Press
When Heaven Invades Earth	Bill Johnson	Treasure House
Knowledge of the Holy	A. W. Tozer	O. M. Publishing
The Pleasures of Loving God	Mike Bickle	Creation House
Manifest Presence	Jack Hayford	Chosen

Title	Author	Publisher
Living the Spirit-Formed Life	Jack Hayford	Regal
The Agape Road	Bob Mumford	Lifechangers
The Sensitivity of the Spirit	R. T. Kendall	Hodder & Stroughton
Living in the Freedom of the Spirit	Tom Marshall	Sovereign World
Secrets of the Secret Place	Bob Sorge	Oasis House
The Heart of Worship	Matt Redman	Regal
Experiencing the Depths of Jesus Christ	Jeanne Guyon	Seedsowers
The Unsurrendered Soul	Liberty Savard	Bridge-Logos
Keys to Heaven's Economy	Shawn Bolz	NewType
Translating God	Shawn Bolz	NewType
Growing up With God	Shawn Bolz	NewType
God Secrets	Shawn Bolz	NewType
Breakthrough, Prophecies, Prayer & Declarations	Shawn Bolz	NewType
Exploring the Prophetic; 90 Day Devotional	Shawn Bolz	NewType
Modern Prophets	Shawn Bolz	NewType
Your Prophetic Life Map	Steve Witt	Emanate Books

ABOUT THE PROPHETIC EQUIPPING SERIES

Graham began teaching prophetic schools in 1986. Eight years later, he wrote *Developing Your Prophetic Gifting*, a book which has won universal acclaim. Translated into numerous languages, reprinted many times over, and published by several companies, it has been a best seller and widely regarded as a classic. Graham has continued to develop new material each year in the Schools of Prophecy. Now, after almost twenty years of teaching and continuously upgrading material, the School of Prophecy has developed into one of the finest teaching programs on the prophetic gift, ministry, and office of a prophet. This new material effectively makes *Developing Your Prophetic Gifting* redundant.

The Prophetic Equipping Series is an ongoing writing project that combines classic teaching with the journal format so popular in the *Being with God Series*. It also embraces training assignments, worshops, and reflective exercises, with emphasis on producing one of the finest teaching aids on the prophetic gift and ministry. These manuals are appropriate for individual, small group or church-wide use. All Christians can prophesy and would benefit from Graham's wisdom and experience in ministry. The assignments, exercises, workshops, lectio divina and other material are designed to further the understanding of the prophetic gift, ministry and office. If used properly, the process will develop accountability for prophetic people, healthy pastoring of the prophetic, and give relevant questions for leadership and prophetic people to ask one another.

ABOUT THE AUTHOR

Graham Cooke and his wife Theresa live in Santa Barbara where they guide and interact with several communities that are millennial, entreprenurial, and focused on the city.

Graham has a leadership and consulting role in a variety of groups and organizations at regional, national, and international levels. He is a mentor to ministries and works in various think tanks to promote Kingdom initiatives.

Theresa has a passion for worship and dance. She loves intercession, cares about injustice and abuse, and has compassion for those who are sick, suffering and disenfranchised.

Together, they have two sons, three daughters and eight grandchildren! They also have two other daughters in Australia who are part of their extended family.

Graham is involved in three aspects of ministry, each of which has a business model attached. These are:

BrilliantPerspectives.com - The consulting and training group that produces a range of messages across the spectrum of life in Christ, church development and Kingdom engagement.

BrilliantBookHouse.com - The online resource for the physical and digital production of all Graham's messages, conferences and school series, plus all his books and propheitc soaking words that have had a profound impact on individuals, familes and churches around the world.

BrilliantTV.com - Our online streaming platform with thousands of subscribers receiving constant, consistent discipleship training and personal development input through a curated online community that is worldwide.

Graham is a popular conference speaker and is well known for his training programs on the prophetic, spiritual warfare, intimacy and devotional life, leadership, spirituality and the church in transition. He functions as a consultant and freethinker to businesses, churches, and organizations, enabling them to develop strategically. He has a passion to establish the Kingdom and build prototype churches that can fully reach a postmodern society.

A strong part of Graham's ministry is in producing finances and resources to the poor and disenfranchised in developing countries. He supports many projects specifically for widows, orphans, and people in the penal system. He hates abuse of women and works actively against human trafficking and the sex slave trade, including women caught up in prostitution and pornography.

If you would like to invite Graham to minister or speak at an event, please complete the online Ministry Invitation Form at www. GrahamCooke.com.